STRIKE A MATCH

21 DAY DEVOTIONAL JOURNAL
THE CATALYST TO SPARKING A FIRE IN MY SOUL

Author: Sandy Study

Graphic Designer: Jessica Harbold

Bible references from biblegateway.com | Quotes from brainyquote.com

HOW TO USE THIS DEVOTION

1. Strike A Match and light your candle

2. Let fragrance fill your reading area

3. Speak the affirmation

4. Read the text

5. Answer the questions

6. Reflect on the verse

7. Journal your own prayer (love note) to God

"The Lord is my light and my salvation— so why should I be afraid? The Lord is my fortress, protecting me from danger, so why should I tremble?"
Psalms 27:1 NLT

"I take joy in doing your will, my God, for your instructions are written on my heart."
Psalms 40:8 NLT

"I love you, Lord, my strength."
Psalms 18:1 NIV

Thank you for taking the time to spark a fire in your heart and your faith. This devotion is designed to be a personal affirmation and to set an atmosphere where your heart can worship, and your mind can be refreshed and challenged. "Strike A Match" is a passion project of 21 vital truths revealed to me along my journey of faith, which has effectively changed my life beautifully. I have ventured out of my comfort zone to share these personal revelations with you. I pray you will hear the heart of God as you read and meditate over each of the daily devotions. Strike a Match, a candle symbolizes hope and light; start a fire in your soul, and see what God can do. Let this time awaken your senses to what God is saying to you personally. You are a light, your devotion time a sweet fragrance, and your prayer a love note to God.

PART 1

BEING ME; **BEING ENOUGH**

STRIKE A MATCH DEVOTION

The catalyst to starting a fire in my soul

STRIKE

/strik/

To ignite, to produce a spark;

MATCH

/maCH/

It is a simple tool to create a spark to start a fire.

DEVOTION

/dəˈvōSH(ə)n/

An observance that can include prayer, reading, and writing;
a source of reflective thoughtfulness to improve one's well-being.

ENOUGH

/iˈnəf/

As much or as many as required for an intended purpose...

BEING ME, BEING ENOUGH

Being me is being enough. I possess gifts and talents more than enough,
I will embrace all that I possess and my potential to be all I have been created
to be.

 I am enough.

"You are good enough, exactly as you are — so go out and do amazing things!"
- Unknown

DAY 1
STRIKE A MATCH; BEING ME; BEING ENOUGH
GOOD ENOUGH

Being me is being enough. I possess gifts and talents, more than enough. I will embrace all that I possess and my potential to be all I have been created to be. I am enough.

The first family, not talking about the POTUS and his clan, but the first people to be on this earth, Adam and Eve. God, the first matchmaker, made Adam and Eve the power couple of the Garden of Eden. In the opening scene of the Bible, their arrival on earth was the miraculous, well-thought-out grand finale to God's six-day creation account. God spoke, and there was light; then the heavens and the earth; sea and the land with vegetation; the sun, moon and stars, then the fish, birds, and animals; and He saw that it was good. The last day of creation was different. God was done speaking things into existence; he took extra care that day and put his hands to work. God imagined what could reflect His image, then got down in the dirt and began to sculpt. For a short time, His masterpiece existed as a pile of dirt.

The sculptor didn't think about the mess creating humans would make. He thought more of the deep connection He would have with His mud pie masterpiece. Then came something that transformed dirt into something extraordinary: the breath of God. **Strike A Match**, God took a deep breath and exhaled his essence and presence, bringing life to His best work, human beings. God created humans in his image, and his essence and presence became integrated into every human fiber. The result is a beautiful, complex, soulful, physical, intellectual, emotional, creative, and adventurous one-of-a-kind living person. "Then God looked over all he had made, and he saw that it was very good" (Gen 1:31). It was good enough for God.

"How are you?"

"I'm good, and you?"

"I'm good."

That is the end of the conversation, the cordial and nice ties, check! Honestly, such a type of exchange is more often a mutual understanding of "I'm not going to tell you how things are, so let's just agree to accept 'good' and move along because my agenda is simply to survive the day, agreed!" In our world of casual conversations, the word "good" has been demoted to meaning "not great", or "a little better than okay". That is not the essence of good; it's synonyms: exceptional, outstanding and magnificent; that is what God meant when he created us, mortal and messy humans. He did and continues to put his hand to work in our lives every day, digging down into our turmoil soil, some of which we have created, to show us and to give us understanding that we are good enough. What God deposited inside us is enough. Each of us is a one-of-a-kind masterpiece, filled with ideas, heart passions, wonder and brilliant thoughts. You already possess what is good enough to face your day, good enough to believe in yourself, and good enough to succeed. God looked at you; he knew that it was good; You are good enough for God. Being me is being enough. I possess gifts and talents that are more than enough, and I will embrace all that I possess, all my potential, to be all that I have been created to be. I am enough.

DAY 1

GOOD ENOUGH

What are your "strike the match" take-a-way points?

What does it mean that you are God's "mud pie masterpiece"?

How will you approach your days knowing that you are good enough?

SO, GOD CREATED HUMAN BEINGS IN HIS OWN IMAGE THEN GOD BLESSED THEM AND SAID, "BE FRUITFUL AND MULTIPLY. FILL THE EARTH AND GOVERN IT. REIGN OVER THE FISH IN THE SEA, THE BIRDS IN THE SKY, AND ALL THE ANIMALS THAT SCURRY ALONG THE GROUND."
THEN GOD SAID, "LOOK! I HAVE GIVEN YOU EVERY SEED - BEARING PLANT THROUGHO UT THE EARTH AND ALL THE FRUIT TREES FOR YOUR FOOD. AND I HAVE GIVEN EVERY GREEN PLANT AS FOOD FOR ALL THE WILD ANIMALS, THE BIRDS IN THE SKY, AND THE SMALL ANIMALS THAT SCURRY ALONG THE GROUND—EVERYTHING THAT HAS LIFE."
THEN GOD LOOKED OVER ALL HE HAD MADE, AND HE SAW THAT IT WAS VERY GOOD! GENESIS 1:27-31 THEN THE LORD GOD FORMED THE MAN FROM THE DUST OF THE GROUND. HE BREATHED THE BREATH OF LIFE INTO THE MAN'S NOSTRILS, AND THE MAN BECAME A LIVING PERSON.

GENESIS 2:7

BEING ME, BEING ENOUGH

DAY 1 | *GOOD ENOUGH*

Dear Lord,

"Whatever you want in life, other people are going to want it too. Believe in yourself enough to accept the idea that you have an equal right to it."
- Diane Sawyer

DAY 2
STRIKE A MATCH; BEING ME; BEING ENOUGH
SIGNIFICANT ENOUGH

Being me is being enough. I possess gifts and talents, more than enough. I will embrace all that I possess and my potential to be all I have been created to be. I am enough.

Well, well, well, what do we have here?

That could have been the dialog, but it wasn't. It could have been silence, a display of discrimination and disregard, but it wasn't. It could have been scandalous, but it wasn't. It was a significant encounter, an exchange that interrupted a normal daily chore for a Samaritan woman. During these times, social tensions ran deep between the Samaritans and the Jewish people, not to mention that it was improper for a woman of ill repute and a rabbi to be seen together, even if it was at Jacob's well, the local source of water.

This particular woman had many layers to her story, making her the talk of the town, and it wasn't because she was running for the school board. Her tainted past included five different husbands and now a new guy, forcing her to retrieve water from the well in the heat of the day. Most ladies came in the cool of the morning, but to avoid the glares of disapproval and the whispers of condemnation that were carried with them like jugs of water, high noon at the well was her safe time. This day, her safe time intersected with a significant time; the Jewish teacher was there to see her.

Strike A Match, "If you only knew the gift God has for you..." Jesus asked for a drink of water, but what he wanted was to give something that no one else could give: a new reputation. He revealed to this Samaritan woman who he was, the Messiah. He knew about her past, her mistakes and about the unkind words spoken that took root in her soul, but he chose to meet her at the well. Suddenly, an exchange of words turned a shame-filled woman into a divine spokesperson. The entire town of haters heard of her significant encounter and saw a significant transformation because The Messiah revealed her significant during His mission on earth.

Glancing into a mirror, we could say the same. "Well, well, well, look who we have here!" The dialog of shame, unkind words, and past mistakes glare right back at us. We don't see anything significant and allow a skewed self-perspective to dictate our days, weeks and eventually years. How much time have we wasted? How many excuses have we made to justify isolation and to remain in the depths of our well, well, well? Suddenly, the revelation of "if you only knew the gifts God has for you" is an encounter of significance; it is your high noon well moment; he chooses to be there with you (where you currently find yourself). That moment can turn anything around; that moment can spark a divine new life and a divine new mission that He chooses you to do. You are significant enough. Being me is being enough. I possess gifts and talents, more than enough, I will embrace all that I possess, all my potential, and be all I have been created to be. I am enough.

DAY 2

STRIKE A MATCH; BEING ME; BEING ENOUGH
SIGNIFICANT ENOUGH

What are your "strike the match" take-a-way
points?

What does it mean to you to know that you are
significant and that you have the same
opportunity to be divinely chosen?

How can you embrace your significance?

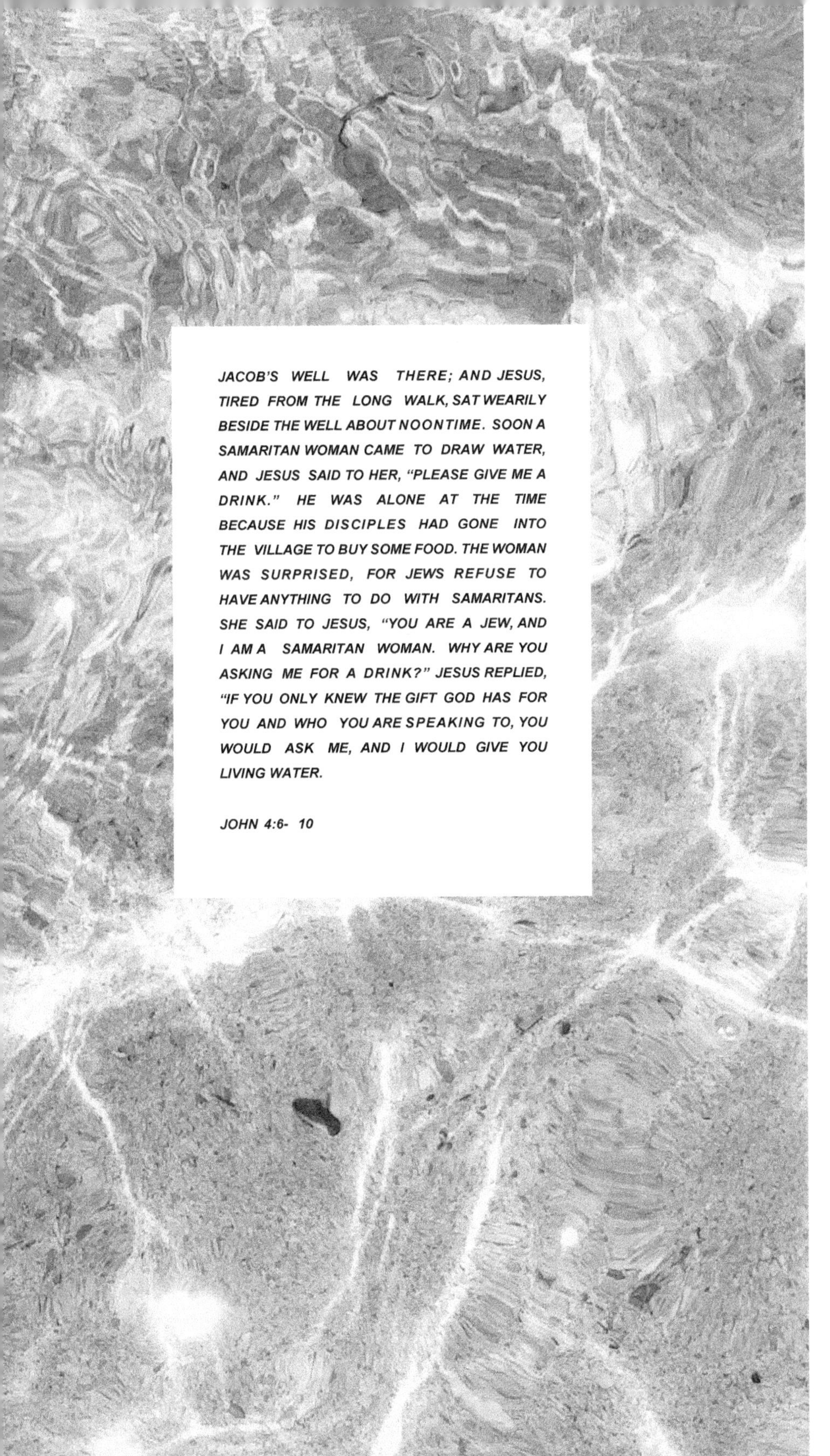
JACOB'S WELL WAS THERE; AND JESUS, TIRED FROM THE LONG WALK, SAT WEARILY BESIDE THE WELL ABOUT NOONTIME. SOON A SAMARITAN WOMAN CAME TO DRAW WATER, AND JESUS SAID TO HER, "PLEASE GIVE ME A DRINK." HE WAS ALONE AT THE TIME BECAUSE HIS DISCIPLES HAD GONE INTO THE VILLAGE TO BUY SOME FOOD. THE WOMAN WAS SURPRISED, FOR JEWS REFUSE TO HAVE ANYTHING TO DO WITH SAMARITANS. SHE SAID TO JESUS, "YOU ARE A JEW, AND I AM A SAMARITAN WOMAN. WHY ARE YOU ASKING ME FOR A DRINK?" JESUS REPLIED, "IF YOU ONLY KNEW THE GIFT GOD HAS FOR YOU AND WHO YOU ARE SPEAKING TO, YOU WOULD ASK ME, AND I WOULD GIVE YOU LIVING WATER.
JOHN 4:6- 10

BEING ME, BEING ENOUGH

DAY 2 | *SIGNIFICANT ENOUGH*

Dear Lord,

____

____

____

____

____

____

____

____

____

____

____

____

"Failure will never overtake me if my determination to succeed is strong enough."
- Og Mandino

DAY 3
STRIKE A MATCH; BEING ME; BEING ENOUGH
STRONG ENOUGH

Being me is being enough. I possess gifts and talents, more than enough. I will embrace all that I possess and my potential to be all I have been created to be. I am enough.

It must have been the most gruesome sight. It was not unusual for crowds of people to push through the narrow ancient streets and jockeying for a position to get close to Jesus, but this day was different. A lack of understanding clouded the thought process of the masses and those closest to him; nothing made sense. The guilty verdict carried a consequence of death for the teacher that continually drew a crowd. What was he guilty of?

He was guilty of being what He was created to be, being The Son of God, the channel of God's love from heaven and earth. The evidence was overwhelming, and he was convicted only because of his love and compassion for all people. The scene shows a severely physically beaten and weakened man, carrying a cross, staggering to his fate and his purpose. It didn't seem as if he was going to make it on his own strength.

Simon, a man in the crowd, was forced to help, walk alongside and carry the weight of the cross Jesus had been carrying. **Strike A Match**, did the son of God need help to fulfill his purpose? How could that be? He should have been strong enough to do it on his own. Was he not who he claimed to be as he needed help? Was he a failure because someone had to walk the Via Dolorosa with him? No, his purpose was outlined from conception to death, all of it; the love journey wasn't easy, and his life to the final hours was not easy. God gave him strength, but when Jesus needed it most, God gave him help. When Simon picked up the cross, Jesus did not refuse the help. God's love for His son and all of mankind was being revealed, even Jesus had help to complete what he came to earth to do, to be the evidence of God's love.

How often do we buy into the lie or have a lack of understanding of what it means to be strong enough? We surmise that we are not and cannot be capable of being who we are created to be. The journey isn't easy; it is a complicated love endeavor, loving God, loving ourselves, and loving others. How often do we proclaim, "I have had enough!" This is a hard stop, mentally, physically, and emotionally. It is a surrender to a lie that we are not strong enough to fulfill our purpose as a spouse, parent, caregiver, employee, entrepreneur, or in our ministry or philanthropic work. Jesus didn't stop; he didn't surrender, the love and compassion he had for the people around him was his purpose, no matter how horrific. God has outlined your purpose from conception to death. You are strong enough to walk out your life and love journey, it is not always easy. There are times when you will feel strong enough, and there will be times when the weight will be too much to bear. In those moments, God will send you help, someone to walk alongside to help bear the burden physically, mentally and emotionally. Don't refuse the help that God will send; it will be the evidence of God's love and compassion for you. You are strong enough. Speak aloud, "Being me is being enough. I possess gifts and talents which are more than enough. I will embrace all that I possess and my potential to be all I have been created to be. I am enough.

D A Y 3
STRIKE A MATCH; BEING ME; BEING ENOUGH
STRONG ENOUGH

What are your "strike the match" take-a-way points?

What does it mean to you to know that you are strong enough to walk out your life and love journey?

How can you embrace the help God sends to you?

AND THEY COMPEL ONE PASSING BY, SIMON OF
CYRENE, COMING FROM THE COUNTRY, THE
FATHER OF ALEXANDER AND RUFUS, TO GO
[WITH THEM], THAT HE MIGHT BEAR
HIS(JESUS') CROSS.AND THEY BRING HIM
UNTO THE PLACE GOLGOTHA, WHICH IS,
BEING INTERPRETED, THE PLACE OF A
SKULL. AND THEY OFFERED HIM WINE
MINGLED WITH MYRRH: BUT HE RECEIVED
IT NOT. AND THEY CRUCIFY HIM,

MARK 15:21-24A ASV

BEING ME, BEING ENOUGH
DAY 3 | *STRONG ENOUGH*

Dear Lord,

"Give me a lever long enough and a fulcrum on which to place it, and I shall move the world."
- Archimedes

DAY 4
STRIKE A MATCH; BEING ME; BEING ENOUGH
CONFIDENT ENOUGH

Being me is being enough. I possess gifts and talents, more than enough. I will embrace all that I possess and my potential to be all I have been created to be. I am enough.

"No, he is not the one next. Do you have another son?"

Samuel, the prophet, repeated this line seven times as he was following the Lord's instructions to find Israel's future king. David, the youngest son of Jesse, was going about his daily chores tending the sheep, and had not even been invited to the future king lineup. Who would have guessed the overlooked youngest, David, would become the guest of honor at the spirit-filled pre-coronation ceremony that day? The next day, he was back to tending sheep in the wilderness. That sounds crazy, but God had more for David to learn. David's confidence in God had to define his character, and his character had to support his God-given calling. I would have loved to follow David on social media; he was probably singing "Lions and tigers and bears, oh my!" as a true influencer of his time. Living as a "Survivor" participant, he hunted down lions and bears that came looking for lamb chops; his choice of weapons was a staff and a slingshot. One day, he was tasked with taking food to his older brothers on the frontlines of Saul's Army. This day is when David's confidence and character would go on display. For forty days, a mighty and large enemy warrior, Goliath, taunted Saul's entire army and challenged a one-on-one, winner-take-all battle. No one stepped up; fear and doubt plagued the ranks. **Strike A Match**, "Uber Eats" David arrives on the scene, but food delivery is not his purpose; facing a giant enemy warrior was, saving a nation was, and stepping into kingship was ordained for that day. He accepted the challenge that trained soldiers wouldn't, which caused special ops to cower and caused the current king, Saul, to be militarily paralyzed on the battlefield. That day, all that God showed David, all his experience and all he had learned tending the flock, protecting the flock and fighting for the flock was for a much greater purpose. When no one else knew what to do, David did, he refused standard issue armor; his armor was unseen; his weapons, that of a boy; his stature small, but his faith large. Confidently, he stepped out, declaring who God was and who his God said he was. One day, one stone hit one giant, and that one day made all of the challenges and preparation in the wilderness clear.

I should, well, maybe I shouldn't. Let's list the pros and cons. What are all the possible outcomes? The inconclusive cycle of micro-analysis can be mentally paralyzing, leading to the decision of indecision. That is where an entire army found themselves, and that is exactly the hard place we can often find ourselves. The blockade, the stalemate, not only to the entire army but to his dream and the anointed promise of God. David had to decide the armor he would wear. Would he wear faith, confidence, and truth, or would he wear the standard issue attire? He decided, and so must we. We were created for more than wearing the standard issue: fear, defeat, and anxiety. David decided to use a slingshot and 5 stones during his one-on-one battle with Goliath. The giant didn't stay standing when one stone laced with faith, confidence and truth was hurled at him, and neither will your giants. The things God has anointed you for are things only you can do. You have been preparing all of your life for the one day that confidence, character and calling collide. One day, things become undeniably ordained when you step out and know what you need to do, even when no one else understands. That day, no giant will stand in the way of your dream and God's promise to you. You are confident. Being me is being enough. I possess gifts and talents, more than enough. I will embrace all that I possess and my potential to be all I have been created to be. I am enough.

D A Y 4

CONFIDENT ENOUGH

What are your "strike the match" take-a-way points?

What giants are you facing?

What life experience will help you face your giants
and stand in faith and confidence?

HE PICKED UP FIVE SMOOTH STONES FROM A STREAM AND PUT THEM INTO HIS SHEPHERD'S BAG. THEN, ARMED ONLY WITH HIS SHEPHERD'S STAFF AND SLING, HE STARTED ACROSS THE VALLEY TO FIGHT THE PHILISTINE.

1 SAMUEL 17:40 NLT

BEING ME, BEING ENOUGH

DAY 4 | *CONFIDENT ENOUGH*

Dear Lord,

*"When something is important enough,
you do it even if the odds are not in your favor."*
- Elon Musk

DAY 5
STRIKE A MATCH; BEING ME; BEING ENOUGH
QUALIFIED ENOUGH

Being me is being enough. I possess gifts and talents, more than enough. I will embrace all that I possess and my potential to be all I have been created to be.

"Right, this way, fellows, what are you looking for? How can I be of service?" The probable greeting at the door of a prostitute named Rahab in the city of Jericho. However, the men at the door were not the typical clientele; they were spies sent by Joshua, leader of the Israelite Army. Their purpose for being there was not an indecent proposal but a divine reconnaissance mission. The army was going to invade the walled city of Jericho, and Rahab's house was built in that wall... The spies convinced Rahab to work with them, and Rahab set her price, as any shrewd businesswoman would. Rahab played the role of a clueless harlot and sent the king's guards on a wild goose chase while hiding the spies. The spies got a rooftop view, the intel they needed and then escaped by propelling down a rope from an upstairs window. But what did Rahab get? **Strike A Match**, she got a promise, she got hope, and she got a new life. She had the right heart even though she had the wrong profession. The Israelite Army began their march toward the city; Rahab gathered her family inside the house and threw a scarlet rope out of the window to signify her location to the approaching army. The conquering Israelite army never fired a shot; they fired off a shout after marching around the city six times. The seventh-round shout caused the walls to collapse, the fate of the city, destruction, but one house had to remain. The promise to Rahab was to stay in your home, and you will be spared. That day, the walls crumbled, but Rahab's faith and obedience were the foundation of her home and her family's survival. She and her family were welcomed into the ranks of the Israeli people; she became a wife and a mother and the great, great, great grandmother of King David and, ultimately, an ancestor of Jesus. Rahab was qualified simply because she had the right heart, and it was the right time. She was in the right location and acted righteously when the opportunity came knocking at her door. A questionable past does not disqualify destiny.

BEING ME; BEING ENOUGH

Most of us don't believe that we are qualified because we have created a resume of disqualifications. It is a PDF in our minds that we update regularly, give out as self-condemnation, and use as a harness for action.

We choose not to act because we believe three fine-print lies.

1. No one person can make a difference, especially me.

2. It's not the right time, or I'm not in the right place in my life.

3. I have made so many bad decisions; can I even trust myself to act righteously when the opportunity comes knocking?

We justify our disqualifications, but God says we are qualified simply because of faith and obedience. The story of Rahab teaches us that a questionable past will not disqualify destiny; only a lack of faith and disobedience will do that. Will your faith and obedience be the foundation of your family? Will your home stand when things are crumbling all around you? An ordained opportunity will come; let your faith and your supernatural understanding of what God can do guide you. Your obedience can make a difference; it may save the life of someone you love, and it will be a blessing for the generations to come. You are qualified. Being me is being enough. I possess gifts and talents, more than enough. I will embrace all that I possess and my potential to be all I have been created to be. I am enough.

D A Y 5

STRIKE A MATCH; BEING ME; BEING ENOUGH
QUALIFIED ENOUGH

What are your "strike the match" take-a-way points?

What does it mean to you to know you are qualified for your God-given destiny?

What steps will you take to let your supernatural understanding of God guide you?

BY FAITH THE WALLS OF JERICHO FELL DOWN AFTER THEY HAD BEEN ENCIRCLED FOR SEVEN DAYS. BY FAITH RAHAB THE PROSTITUTE DID NOT PERISH WITH THOSE WHO WERE DISOBEDIENT, BECAUSE SHE HAD GIVEN A FRIENDLY WELCOME TO THE SPIES.

HEBREWS 11:30-31 ESV

BEING ME, BEING ENOUGH
DAY5 | *QUALIFIED ENOUGH*

Dear Lord,

"Be as smart as you can, but remember that it is always better to be wise than to be smart."
- Alan Alda

DAY 6
STRIKE A MATCH; BEING ME; BEING ENOUGH
WISE ENOUGH

Being me is being enough. I possess gifts and talents, more than enough. I will embrace all that I possess, all my potential to be all that I have been created to be. I am enough.

At the age of twenty, Solomon, the son of King David, found himself sitting in the throne room with a crown upon his head, the turmoil of family in his heart and the weight of a nation on his shoulders. His father's health was failing, and he was named the one, the next King of Israel. I can only imagine the inner angst that must have been swirling: the palace, the people, the projects, the pressure, the purpose, the promise, all eyes on him. The thought of "This is one big crown to fill", must have hurt his head more than the crown itself. What was he to do with all that he had inherited? He realized he wasn't going to be the King he needed to be unless he heeded his father's charge. Be strong, and show yourself to be a man. And keep the charge of the Lord your God, walking in His ways, keeping His statutes, His commandments, His judgments, and His testimonies, as it is written in the Law of Moses, that you may prosper in all that you do and wherever you turn, (1 Kings 2:2-3 MEV). What to do now? Solomon did the best thing he could do. He put his angst to sleep, and The Lord appeared to him in a dream. God knew what he needed, but He asked Solomon what he wanted, and the conversation began. Solomon humbled himself and shared with God what he was concerned about, "I am just a child…I don't know what to do, and I am here with your chosen people, this great nation…". Solomon asked for a discerning heart and wisdom. **Strike A Match**, he could have asked for anything, any material thing, any military thing, any pleasurable thing, but the thing he asked for was wisdom. Solomon went on to build the temple of the Lord, a place of worship for the God of Israel, a place to house the presence of the Lord for the people of Israel. He became an author and a poet, brokered deals and alliances with other countries and was historically known as one of the wisest kings. God gave him the step-by-step heavenly "how to be a successful king" blueprint simply because he was wise enough to ask for wisdom.

Nope, it can't be that simple. Who can really know about my angst, my palace, people, pressure, and projects? You are so right; you are the only one who can face what you have inherited, and the things that need to be done in your own personal kingdom.

Planning things can be a common thing but have the majority of us taken into consideration planning for personal success, being proactive instead of reactive to what our daily lives throw at us?

Solomon recognized his life, though extremely blessed; it was not going to be a walk in the palace courtyard. Neither is ours. He knew what he needed more than anything, and it was a discerning heart and Godly wisdom.

We are in the information age, but there is no situation that you will find yourself in that God doesn't have the answer for, but for some reason, we will still ask Google before we ask God. Maybe you didn't have God appear in a dream, but you do have direct access to Him through prayer. God knows what you need, and He knows the angst that keeps you up at night. He knows the promises He has given you and the purpose of it all. He has the "how to be a successful you" blueprint; the only thing you have to do is ask for it, and a discerning heart and wisdom are freely given. You are wise enough to ask. Being me is being enough. I possess gifts and talents, more than enough. I will embrace all that I possess, all my potential to be all that I have been created to be. I am enough.

D A Y 6
STRIKE A MATCH; BEING ME; BEING ENOUGH
WISE ENOUGH

What are your "strike the match" take-a-way points?

What situations are you facing right now that you need wisdom for?

What peace do you have knowing that God has a "how to be a successful you" blueprint ready for you?

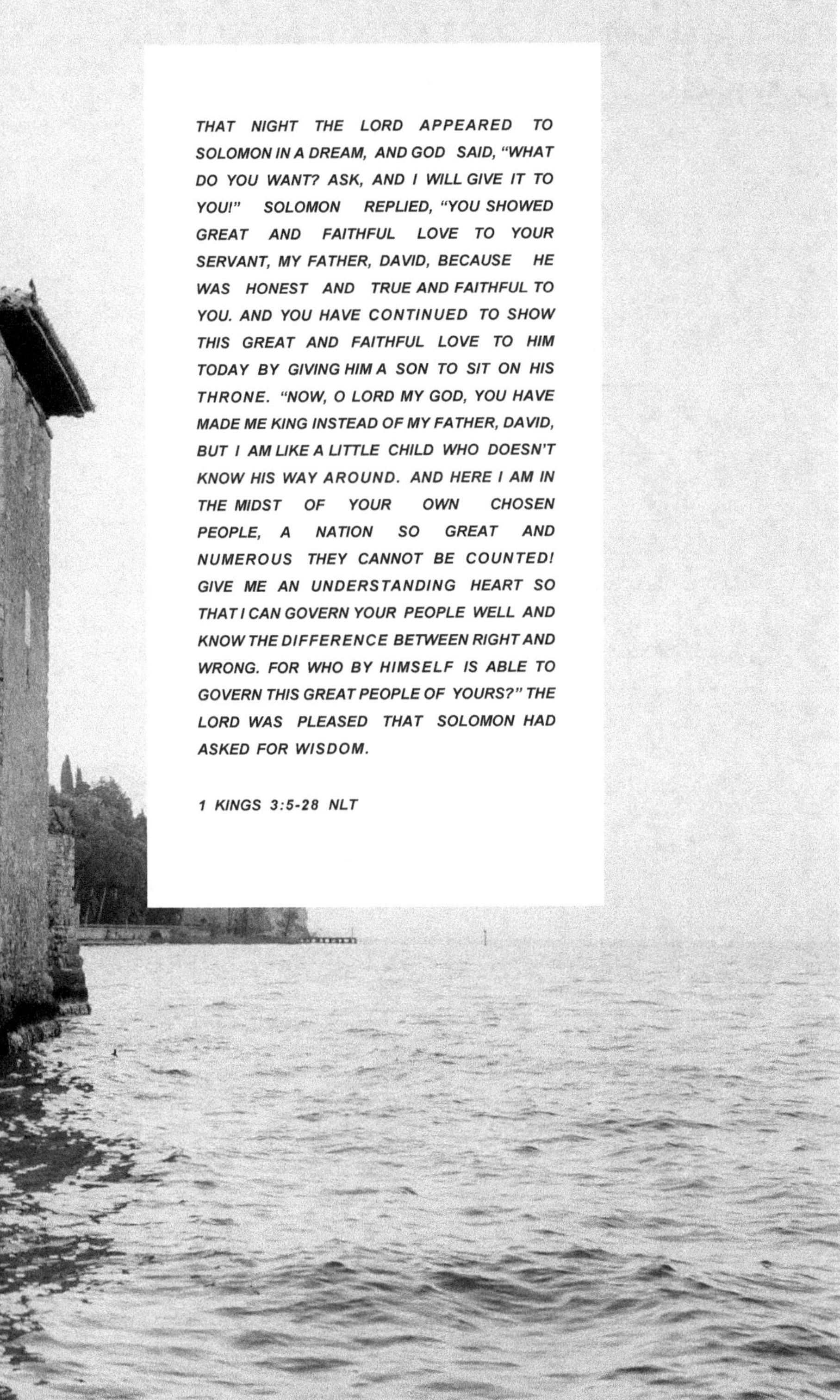

THAT NIGHT THE LORD APPEARED TO SOLOMON IN A DREAM, AND GOD SAID, "WHAT DO YOU WANT? ASK, AND I WILL GIVE IT TO YOU!" SOLOMON REPLIED, "YOU SHOWED GREAT AND FAITHFUL LOVE TO YOUR SERVANT, MY FATHER, DAVID, BECAUSE HE WAS HONEST AND TRUE AND FAITHFUL TO YOU. AND YOU HAVE CONTINUED TO SHOW THIS GREAT AND FAITHFUL LOVE TO HIM TODAY BY GIVING HIM A SON TO SIT ON HIS THRONE. "NOW, O LORD MY GOD, YOU HAVE MADE ME KING INSTEAD OF MY FATHER, DAVID, BUT I AM LIKE A LITTLE CHILD WHO DOESN'T KNOW HIS WAY AROUND. AND HERE I AM IN THE MIDST OF YOUR OWN CHOSEN PEOPLE, A NATION SO GREAT AND NUMEROUS THEY CANNOT BE COUNTED! GIVE ME AN UNDERSTANDING HEART SO THAT I CAN GOVERN YOUR PEOPLE WELL AND KNOW THE DIFFERENCE BETWEEN RIGHT AND WRONG. FOR WHO BY HIMSELF IS ABLE TO GOVERN THIS GREAT PEOPLE OF YOURS?" THE LORD WAS PLEASED THAT SOLOMON HAD ASKED FOR WISDOM.

1 KINGS 3:5-28 NLT

BEING ME, BEING ENOUGH
DAY 6 | *WISE ENOUGH*

Dear Lord,

____

____

____

____

____

____

____

____

____

____

____

____

____

"The ones who are crazy enough to think that they can change the world are the ones who do."
- John McAfee

DAY 7
STRIKE A MATCH; BEING ME; BEING ENOUGH
CRAZY ENOUGH

Being me is being enough. I possess gifts and talents, more than enough. I will embrace all that I possess, all my potential to be all that I have been created to be. I am enough.

Just out for a walk on a snowy day, maybe... I'm not sure what Benaiah was doing. Was he checking his hunting traps, or was this mighty warrior out on a routine security patrol for the Israeli army? One can only speculate why the details are untold, but this random, obscure passage is recorded nevertheless.
Let's just say Benaiah was out on paw patrol, and it was going to be a snowy adventure like never before. From what scripture reports, Benaiah never backed down; he faced every challenge head-on, and this day was no different. He found himself in a pit. The thing is, he was not alone. As he looked around, big reflective eyes glared back at him, deep growls echoed in the dark chamber and in an instant, paws the size of dinner plates were running full speed toward him. In an instant, his whole life played out like a short YouTube eulogy.

Was this the end, or was it just the beginning of something great? His choices face the lion that wanted to devour him or become the lion's mane course (yes, a little play on words there). Did he fall into a desperate situation, or did he fall into a divine appointment with a lion? God wired Benaiah to be a warrior, and Benaiah knew exactly who he was, who God created him to be, and he had a lion-slayer perspective. **Strike A Match**, Benaiah was crazy enough to believe in a big God, crazy enough to believe that he was a part of God's big plan, and so Benaiah responded big, going into action in a pit on a snowy day. The roar was loud, and the claws sharp but the strength of the lion was no match for the strength of the warrior inside of Benaiah. A non-threatening lifeless lion and a victorious Benaiah were all that was left after the pit match. That event is recorded in the hearts and minds of the soldiers and in the courts of King David.

It was the beginning. Benaiah went on to be one of the three most trusted advisors to King David'; he was the head of King David's secret service, commanded the king's mercenaries, he carried out the dying wishes of King David, ensuring Solomon as predecessor to the throne, and then becomes commander over King Solomon's Army.

Just out for a walk on a snowy day, no, it was a fall into a divine appointment.

What is the craziest thing you almost did in obedience to God? What is the kindest thing you almost did in obedience to God? In an instance we make a choice to believe or not to believe in a big God and God's big plan for our life. A lion-slayer perspective is directly related to how big God is viewed personally. How you view God will determine how you see yourself, and how you see yourself will determine how you respond to God. How you respond to God will determine who you will become.

To find that personal perspective, we each have to face the lions in the pit, the lion that glares intimidation, that roars "wimp" instead of "warrior", and has paws that try to swipe away opportunity. The thing is, it is a risk; it seems crazy to go mentally toe to paw against those lions, and put crazy big action to that risk, but how big is your God? What is at risk if we do not take the risk?

 Crazy, big actions stretch our faith and our thinking. When we allow God to stretch us, we get a new experience leading us to a new life perspective, showing how big God really is. That is God's cycle for building your faith and future, your greatest opportunity might be behind the lion you slay. You are crazy enough to be obedient to a big God. Being me is being enough. I possess gifts and talents, more than enough. I will embrace all that I possess, all my potential to be all that I have been created to be. I am enough.

D A Y 7
STRIKE A MATCH; BEING ME; BEING ENOUGH
CRAZY ENOUGH

What are your "strike the match" take-a-way points?

How big is God to you?

How can you embrace a lion slayer perspective, knowing it is risky but knowing you are a part of God's big plan?

BENAIAH SON OF JEHOIADA, A VALIANT FIGHTER FROM KABZEEL, PERFORMED GREAT EXPLOITS. HE STRUCK DOWN MOAB'S TWO MIGHTIEST WARRIORS. HE ALSO WENT DOWN INTO A PIT ON A SNOWY DAY AND KILLED A LION.

2 SAMUEL 23:20 NIV

BEING ME, BEING ENOUGH
DAY 7 | *CRAZY ENOUGH*

Dear Lord,

PART 2

BEING ME; **BEING FREE**

STRIKE A MATCH DEVOTION

The catalyst to starting a fire in my soul

STRIKE

/strik/

To ignite, to produce a spark;

MATCH

/maCH/

A simple tool used to create a spark to start a fire.

DEVOTION

/də ˈvōSH(ə)n/

An observance that can include prayer, reading, and writing;
a source of reflective thoughtfulness to improve one's well-being.

FREE

/frē/

Not under the control or in the power of another; able to act or be done as
one wishes. Not limited in any way.

BEING ME, BEING FREE

Being me is being free; I am free to be me, the me God has created me to be.

I let go of the thoughts and things that hold me back, and I embrace being me,
being free. I am free.

"I would like to be remembered as a person who wanted to be free... so other people would be also free."
- Rosa Parks

DAY 1
STRIKE A MATCH; BEING ME; BEING FREE
FREE TO BE ME

Being me is being free; I am free to be me, the me God has created me to be.

I let go of the thoughts and things that hold me back, and I embrace being me. I am free.

Who did all this? What was her name? It was Miriam, an obscure Old Testament character enslaved in Egypt for 86 years. Though a Hebrew woman, born a slave, living in hardship, and in circumstances beyond her control, she pursued an attitude of inner freedom. Her Strike A Match story is short; her moment in the limelight, 'fleeting', but her purpose, 'undeniable'. She orchestrated freedom, prepared for freedom, and witnessed true Freedom in her life.

As the older sister of Moses, Miriam orchestrated freedom, she saved her baby brother from a decree to execute all Hebrew boys that was issued by the Pharaoh of Egypt. As a young girl, she placed her younger brother in a basket and floated him down the Nile (just a thought, but it doesn't seem like a plausible solution to the problem). However, Moses was rescued by the pharaoh's daughter, raised and educated in Pharaoh's palace, eventually becoming the man God used to negotiate the release of his family and all of the Hebrew people from slavery...

Miriam prepared for freedom. The day finally came, Miriam packed her essentials, and a tambourine and all the Hebrew people walked out of 400 years of Egyptian bondage. Upon seeing the mass exodus of the laborers that built the grand structures of his empire, Pharaoh changed his mind and gave chase to the liberated slaves. It seemed their short-lived freedom would end in death, but the story was not over; the epic plot twist was yet to be revealed. **Strike A Match**, suddenly, Miriam witnessed freedom, the ripple effect of what she did as a young girl. She watched as her baby brother, Moses, now 80 years of age, held up his staff. The waters of the Red Sea began to separate, and walls of water were created. A natural obstacle was now a miraculous dry path to freedom. When all the Hebrew people had crossed into a new land on the other side, they watched as the Egyptian army was engulfed by the returning waters of the sea. She knew in her heart that God's people were meant to be free.

Though years had passed, she held onto the promise of freedom. Miriam, a woman labeled a slave, decided to be free and prepared to be free long before she witnessed freedom. Miriam knew in her heart she was meant to sing with a tambourine in her hand and dance with no limitations.

I don't know about you; I am not sure my patience and attitude would have held out for 86 years (or if I will even be here when I'm 86). Also, I think I would have grabbed my phone before grabbing a tambourine. I would have thought more of posting about the appearance of freedom, not actually rejoicing in true freedom.

Our lives are dictated by schedules, events, deadlines, and obligations, not to mention the battleground of the brain. Day in and day out our default can be the appearance of having it all together, juggling it all perfectly, all the while not finding that part of us that can dance with no limitations. Our thoughts can be as enslaving as a pharaoh.

Labels that we place upon ourselves will place limitations on what we expect God to do and the freedom He has promised. You are not a slave to your past, your mistakes, your hardships, or your circumstances, so do not label your future by any of those things. You are free to be you and God has created you to be You. It is time for you to dance and sing in your freedom. You are here to orchestrate freedom, witness freedom, and prepare for freedom. How do you prepare for freedom? Decide today, "Being me is being free, I am free to be me, the me God has created me to be. I let go of the thoughts and things that hold me back, and I embrace being me; I am free."

D A Y 1

FREE TO BE ME

What are your "strike the match" take-a-way points?

What are the things that have kept you captive and you need
to decide to be free from?

How will you orchestrate freedom for yourself? If you don't feel free,
do you believe the reason is self-imposed or created by someone else?

THEN MIRIAM THE PROPHET,
AARON'S (AND MOSES')
SISTER, TOOK A
TAMBOURINE AND LED
ALL THE WOMEN AS THEY
PLAYED THEIR TAMBOURINES
AND DANCED. AND MIRIAM
SANG THIS SONG:
"SING TO THE LORD, FOR HE
HAS TRIUMPHED GLORIOUS
LY; HE HAS HURLED BOTH
HORSE AND RIDER INTO THE
SEA."

Exodus 15:20-21

BEING ME; BEING FREE
DAY1 | *FREE TO BE ME,*

Dear Lord,

"To serve is beautiful, but only if it is done with joy and a whole heart and a free mind."

- Pearl S. Buck

DAY 2

STRIKE A MATCH; BEING ME; BEING FREE

FREE TO BE SEEN

Being me is being free; I am free to be me, the me God has created me to be.

I let go of the thoughts and things that hold me back, and I embrace being me; I am free.

In the Old Testament, the wives of wealthy men had maidservants; female domestic help. Hagar found this to be her plot in life; she was a servant to Sarai. She had no status, no volition, no life of her own. In the home of Abram and Sarai, Hagar took care of daily household routines and, at times, unorthodox "chores"(reality television level "chores").

When Sarai could not conceive a child, Hagar was sent as a 'pinch hitter" to attend to the needs of Abram and to provide an heir. The goal was achieved, but the household dynamics became tension-filled, Sarai resentful and scorned, and Hagar frustrated and miserable. Overwhelmed by the circumstances of her life, pregnant, alone and in great despair, Hagar left everything, escaping into the unknown and wandering in the wilderness.

Right before she was ready to give up on her life and the life of her child, an angel of the Lord met her where she was and asked a **Strike A Match** question, "Where have you come from, and where are you going?" This inquiry gripped her heart and gave her a revelation. She had traded one desperate situation for another; running away was not the answer, but what she learned in the wilderness could only be revealed there: truth.

The truth was, she was not overlooked, and God saw her troubles. She returned to her mistress and her purpose. It was not a promise that things would be easy; her circumstances did not change, but her heart and mind did. It was a promise of freedom, freedom from desperate obscurity. Hagar was set free in her mind because she understood her status as "Seen by God".

BEING ME; BEING FREE

It is the oddest thing, in this highly connected world we live in, there are so many people that still feel alone and isolated. Instantly, we are informed of the world around us, headlines of injustice, turmoil and tragedy scroll across our phones, and so retreating into isolation seems more appealing than participating in this imploding world.

Then, the icing on the cake: comparison, causing an over critical evaluation of our daily life. Social media posts the great lives of others, while for some of us, the bar of a great day is measured by the size of the laundry pile; it can be the catalyst to unhealthy comparison and feelings of being unimportant. Sometimes we think just like Hagar, "If I could just escape, get some respite, and run away, things might be better".

The troubling (or the fortunate) thing about running away is we can never run from ourselves or God. "Where have you come from, and where are you going?" That question brings freedom because God knows where you have been, and He cares where you are going. He has brought you through past struggles, He sees you in your current struggle, and He knows those you will face tomorrow.

It is freedom from desperate obscurity, isolation, loneliness, and comparison because you have a new status; "Seen by God". He sees YOU! He sees you as you are and the great inside of you, free to embrace this stage of your life. Embrace today, "Being me is being free. I am free to be me, the me God has created me to be. I let go of the thoughts and things that hold me back, and I embrace being me; I am free."

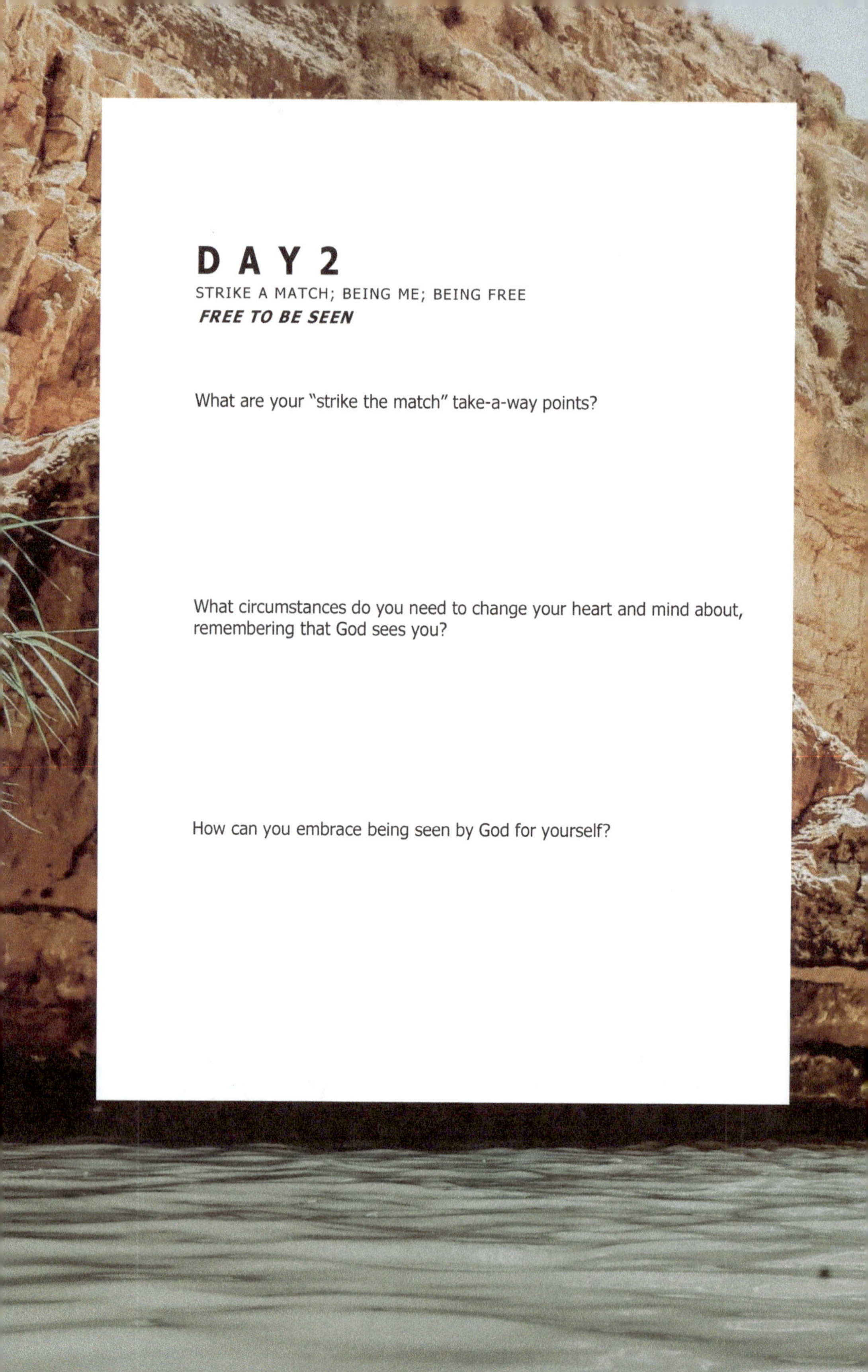

D A Y 2
STRIKE A MATCH; BEING ME; BEING FREE
FREE TO BE SEEN

What are your "strike the match" take-a-way points?

What circumstances do you need to change your heart and mind about, remembering that God sees you?

How can you embrace being seen by God for yourself?

NOW THE ANGEL OF THE LORD FOUND HER BY A SPRING OF WATER IN THE WILDERNESS ... AND HE SAID, "HAGAR, SARAI'S MAID, WHERE HAVE YOU COME FROM, AND WHERE ARE YOU GOING?"... THEREAFTER, HAGAR USED ANOTHER NAME TO REFER TO THE LORD, WHO HAD SPOKEN TO HER. SHE SAID, "YOU ARE THE GOD WHO SEES ME. "SHE ALSO SAID, "HAVE I TRULY SEEN THE ONE WHO SEES ME?

Genesis 16: 7-8,13

BEING ME; BEING FREE
DAY2 | *FREE TO BE SEEN,*

Dear Lord,

"Freedom lies in being bold"- Robert Frost

DAY 3
STRIKE A MATCH; BEING ME; BEING FREE
FREE TO BE BOLD

Being me is being free; I am free to be me, the me God has created me to be. I let go of the thoughts and things that hold me back, and I embrace being me; I am free.

 "Who touched me?" She did. But who was she? An unnamed woman in the scriptures of the New Testament who suffered from a twelve-year-long issue. A twelve-year personal story of coping daily with a physical ailment that made her religiously unclean and socially ostracized. Her issue should have been private, but it was made public; her judgment, 'public', but her pain private.

She was hemorrhaging, hurting physically and mentally, and ashamed; why tell her story? Her story is a story of desperation, desperation to be free of her issue, so much so that she defied "Miss Manner's" editorial suggestions and religious etiquette. She became empowered by the expectation of being free. **Strike A Match**: She was free to be bold, free to walk through the hometown of her judges, push through the crowd, and grab what she needed from that man: healing.

She fell to the ground, not in defeat, but to grab the hem of the Messiah. At that moment, His power confronted her twelve-year personal plague, the issue that kept her from living her best life, the issue that drained every ounce of her finances, physical energy, and mental well-being, left her. Boldly, she thought, and boldly, she acted. She had to answer for her boldness; in trembling, she told the truth to the crowd. What she may have said, "It was me; I touched you." Then the Messiah addressed her and called her a daughter, no longer to be identified as the woman with the issue, but a daughter that could be free and put her issue behind her.

Get the tissues; we all got issues. Some we deal with daily, some are triggered, revealing themselves in ugly moments, and some drain our personal finances, physical energy and mental well-being. To justify whichever issue we currently are manifesting, we use more palatable terms, "retail therapy", "busyness", and "emotional".

The thing is, our personal issues affect the world around us, the people closest to us, and the dialog in our brains. Our life story, how should it be defined, by our issues or by freedom from our issues? You can be empowered by the expectation of being free. Your issue doesn't own you; you have access to power that belongs to you.

Your reach is far greater than you realize, your strength is more powerful than your energy level, and your voice is not something that is given to you but to be boldly used. You are free, free to be bold in your thoughts and actions, to be healed of the issues that are holding you back. "Being me is being free; I am free to be me, the me God has created me to be. I let go of the thoughts and things that hold me back, and I embrace being me; I am free."

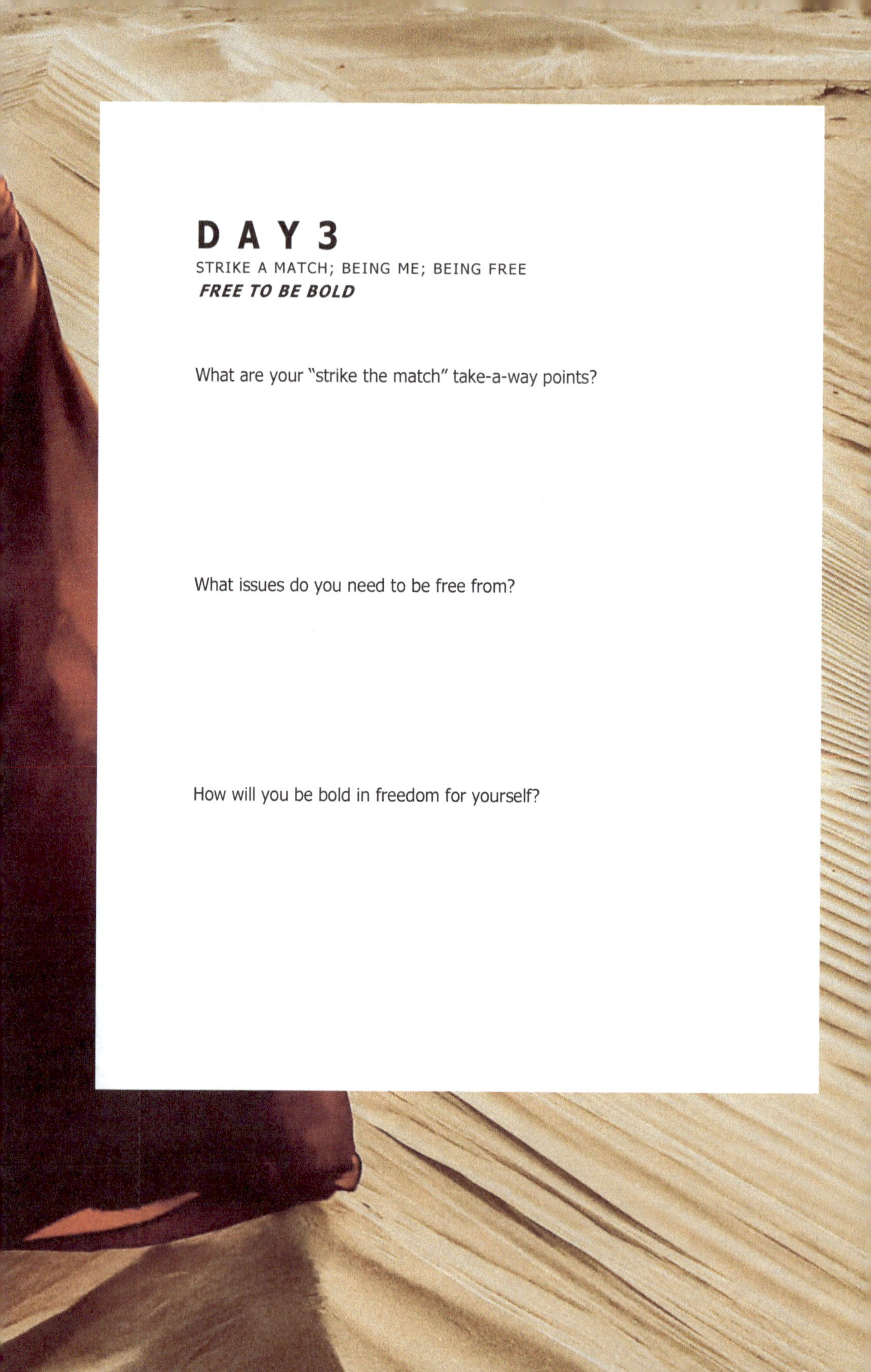

D A Y 3
STRIKE A MATCH; BEING ME; BEING FREE
FREE TO BE BOLD

What are your "strike the match" take-a-way points?

What issues do you need to be free from?

How will you be bold in freedom for yourself?

WHO TOUCHED ME?'" BUT
JESUS KEPT LOOKING AROUND
TO SEE WHO HAD DONE IT.
THEN THE WOMAN, KNOWING
WHAT HAD HAPPENED TO HER,
CAME AND FELL AT HIS FEET
AND, TREMBLING WITH FEAR,
TOLD HIM THE WHOLE TRUTH.
HE SAID TO HER, "DAUGHTER,
YOUR FAITH HAS HEALED YOU.
GO IN PEACE AND BE FREED
FROM YOUR SUFFERING.

Mark 5:31-33

BEING ME; BEING FREE
DAY 3 | *FREE TO BE BOLD,*

Dear Lord,

"I had crossed the line. I was free, but there was no one to welcome me to the land of freedom. I was a stranger in a strange land." -Harriet Tubman.

DAY 4
STRIKE A MATCH; BEING ME; BEING FREE
FREE TO DREAM

Being me is being free; I am free to be me, the me God has created me to be. I let go of the thoughts and things that hold me back, and I embrace being me; I am free.

Jacob, a young man at a turning point in his life, was on the road, trying to find himself and embrace the next season of his life. He ventured out from his parents' home, all the comforts (well, comforts of that period in history), all the security of familiarity, and traveling in search of a wife.

This is just a small part of Jacob's very complex life story, but it was transformative. While on his journey, he became tired, so exhausted he found a stone to rest his head upon (again, I question the standards of comfort) and fell asleep. He wasn't expecting anything but a night's sleep, but he was given a dream. The dream wasn't given in a comfortable place; it was given in a certain place.

He could never imagine the place where his strength was exhausted and he fell and surrendered to sleep on the land that God would give him. **Strike A Match**, he set out to find who he was, apart from his family, and he found his place in this world because he had a dream.

Jacob, even in his weariness, despite a journey that was hot, dusty and tiring, was free to dream. He was free to dream in a land that was unfamiliar. He was free to build that dream, and his dream led to a prosperous life that would benefit many generations to come.

"Some may say you're a dreamer, but you're not the only one" (- The Beatles).

We dream of what we will be when we grow up, we dream of the things to do if we win the Powerball drawing, we dream of finding that one perfect person, and we dream of the places we will venture to and live.

We aren't any different than Jacob; we all experience new seasons in life and the weariness of everyday routines, but even in the exhaustion of seeking and traveling life's journey, we can dream. What does it mean to be free to dream? It means that no matter what place you find yourself in, you have a place in this world, a place that God himself has carved out just for you; you have intellectual property, creativity and novel ingenuity that you are lying on every time you rest your head.

You are free, free to dream, to build and to prosper just as Jacob did. "Being me is being free; I am free to be me, the me God has created me to be. I let go of the thoughts and things that hold me back, and I embrace being me; I am free."

D A Y 4
STRIKE A MATCH; BEING ME; BEING FREE
FREE TO DREAM

What are your "strike the match" take-a-way points?

What dreams do you have?

How will you begin to build your dream?

JACOB FOUND A STONE TO
REST HIS HEAD AGAINST AND
LAY DOWN TO SLEEP. AS HE
SLEPT, HE DREAMED OF A
STAIRWAY THAT REACHED
FROM THE EARTH UP TO
HEAVEN. AND HE SAW THE
ANGELS OF GOD GOING UP AND
DOWN THE STAIRWAY..."I AM
THE LORD, THE GOD OF YOUR
GRANDFATHER ABRAHAM, AND
THE GOD OF YOUR FATHER,
ISAAC. THE GROUND YOU ARE
LYING ON BELONGS TO YOU. I
AM GIVING IT TO YOU AND YOUR
DESCENDANTS.

Genesis 28:11-13

BEING ME; BEING FREE
DAY4 | *FREE TO DREAM,*

Dear Lord,

"The thing you fear most has no power. Your fear of it is what has the power. Facing the truth really will set you free."

-Oprah Winfrey

DAY 5
STRIKE A MATCH; BEING ME; BEING FREE
FREE FROM FEAR

Being me is being free; I am free to be me, the me God has created me to be. I let go of the thoughts and things that hold me back, and I embrace being me; I am free.

'I'm afraid!" Words that no one would think should ever come from his mouth. He, Elijah, was a prophet to the nation of Israel during the reign of King Ahab. King Ahab was a treacherous ruler known for killing the prophets of God and promoting the worship of Baal, practices that included inhuman rituals (in a bad way, probably where "omg" originated).

So, Elijah, the servant of the Lord, faced the king and his treachery head-on. There was a showdown, and Elijah came out on top each time. If he were to be interviewed, his resume is nothing short of miraculous. "Elijah, give an example of when you witnessed the power of God?" The answer: "One time I called fire down from heaven, igniting a Baal incinerating bonfire, and there was another time the King took his chariot to Jezreel. I tucked my tunic in my belt and ran, beating him and his horse to the city gate".

Elijah seemed to have the "it" factor; "it" worked; whatever he did, "it" became a supernatural account of who God was. Something happened, though; the king's wife, Jezebel, a vindictive woman, embarrassed by the bonfire that mocked and discredited her unspeakable worship practices, sent word to Elijah, "You are a dead man!". Fear gripped Elijah, and he ran for his life and hid in a cave, but God wasn't done showing up and showing off. God spoke to Elijah, called him out of the cave, "What are you doing here?" and told him to stand on top of the mountain.

In that moment, God sent a fierce wind that shattered rocks, then the earth quaked, then a great fire, but after the fire came a still small voice; it was the voice of God. That still small voice was the presence of God, **Strike A Match**. God was not in the catastrophe but in the calm.

That voice calms every fear, no matter what is seen with the natural eye, no matter what chaos is surrounding. Listen for that voice. Elijah then understood something that was more important than miraculous events, and he understood miraculous peace. He was free, free from fear, free to live a life directed by the still, small voice that came not from a dark cave but from the top of a mountain.

Guilty, right here, a siren, an unanswered text, an unexpected pain, or footage of a natural disaster can get me from 0 to 100 mph on my fearometer in sixty seconds flat. It becomes irrelevant that yesterday, God blessed me with safety, social connections, good health and beautiful weather. We all have triggers and moments where worst-case scenarios become a dark cave of fearful thoughts. "What are you doing there?" It is not where you belong; don't allow fear to paralyze your journey.

Go to a mental mountain top, get a different view, take a moment, take a deep breath, and listen for that still small voice, the one that brings a miraculous peace. You are free from fear. "Being me is being free, I am free to be me, the me God has created me to be. I let go of the thoughts and things that hold me back and I embrace being me, I am free."

D A Y 5
STRIKE A MATCH; BEING ME; BEING FREE
FREE FROM FEAR

What are your "strike the match" take-a-way points?

What fears do you need to be free from?

How will you listen for that voice that brings miraculous peace?

ELIJAH WAS AFRAID AND
FLED FOR HIS LIFE; HE WENT
INTO A CAVE TO SPEND THE
NIGHT. SUDDEN LY THE
LORD SPOKE TO HIM,
"ELIJAH, WHAT ARE YOU
DOING HERE?" HE
ANSWERED, "LORD GOD
ALMIGHTY, I HAVE ALWAYS
SERVED YOU—YOU ALONE… I
AM THE
ON LY ONE LEFT—AND THEY
ARE TRYING TO KILL ME!" GO
OUT AND STAND BEFORE ME
ON TOP OF THE MOUNTAIN,"
THE LORD SAID TO HIM. THEN
THE LORD PASSED BY AND
SENT A FURIOUS WIND THAT
SPLIT THE HILLS AND
SHATTERED THE ROCKS—
BUT THE LORD WAS NOT IN
THE WIND. THE WIND
STOPPED BLOWING, AND
THEN THERE WAS AN
EARTHQUAKE—BUT THE
LORD WAS NOT IN THE
EARTHQUAKE. AFTER THE
EARTHQUAKE THERE WAS A
FIRE—BUT THE LORD WAS
NOT IN THE FIRE. AND AFTER
THE FIRE THERE WAS THE
SOFT WHISPER OF A VOICE.

1 Kings 19:3,9-12

BEING ME; BEING FREE
DAY 5 | *FREE FROM FEAR,*

Dear Lord,

D A Y 6
STRIKE A MATCH; BEING ME; BEING FREE
FREE TO FORGIVE

Being me is being free; I am free to be me, the me God has created me to be. I let go of the thoughts and things that hold me back, and I embrace being me; I am free.

"Secure all personal items, no standing, keep arms and hands inside the ride at all times, and enjoy the ride", a familiar set of rules explained right before embarking on a gravity defying amusement park ride. Well, that is the only introduction that can be given to the story of Joseph.

His life was a roller coaster of events and situations that took him to the lowest of lows and the highest of highs. The rapid fire highlights of the life of Joseph: he was the beloved son of Jacob (the guy on day 4, free to dream), and he was a dreamer like his father. He had ten mischievous, jealous and vindictive brothers who plotted to kill him, threw him in a pit and then decided the best option was selling him to traveling merchants, telling their father that Joseph met his demise as dinner for a wild animal.

Wait, it gets better; He was then sold to an Egyptian official, Potipher. Joseph worked as a house servant diligently, earning a promotion to manager of the entire household. Not bad, but Potiphar's wife (we'll call her "Hotsy") had something a little extra spicy in mind for Joseph. When Joseph turns down Hotsy's flirtation and seductive ways out of anger, she turns the narrative 360, falsely telling her husband that Joseph came after her.

Well, that chain of events led to Joseph wearing chains in a prison cell. Diligent Joseph strikes again, he is the ideal prisoner, promoted to jailhouse overseer. Joseph councils the other prisoners and even interprets their dreams. As providence would have it, the Pharaoh of Egypt had a troubling dream, and Joseph was the only one who could give an interpretation and wise counsel regarding the impending famine coming to the country.

The result, you guessed it, Joseph became second in command in Egypt. Enter stage right. Joseph's brothers, distraught by the famine, leave home (under the guidance of their father, Jacob) and go to Egypt. The family reunion could have been a knockdown drag-out fight, but that is not who Joseph was; he was diligent in his tasks, but more remarkably, he was diligent in extending a heart of forgiveness. He gave heaping bags of food and saved his family. **Strike A Match**, Joseph's story, fueled forgiveness, not bitterness. He was free to forgive because he recognized what was meant for evil, God meant and turned for good.

What is the roller coaster story that you could give a personal account of? Each of us has highs and lows that could include family drama, manipulation, false accusations, lies, and selfishness, as well as personal triumphs of diligence and promotions. The narrative of the story is all relative to the attitude lens used to look at each event and situation. Joseph and his brothers had a mountain of hurt to overcome, and so did we. We believe that every detail should be hashed out, every opinion voiced, every finger pointed, but it truly all comes down to two things: asking for forgiveness and giving forgiveness. None of the details matter; resolving unrelenting discord is all that matters. When a heart of forgiveness is extended, bitterness is released. Your story can fuel forgiveness. You are free, free to forgive. "Being me is being free; I am free to be me, the me God has created me to be. I let go of the thoughts and things that hold me back, and I embrace being me; I am free."

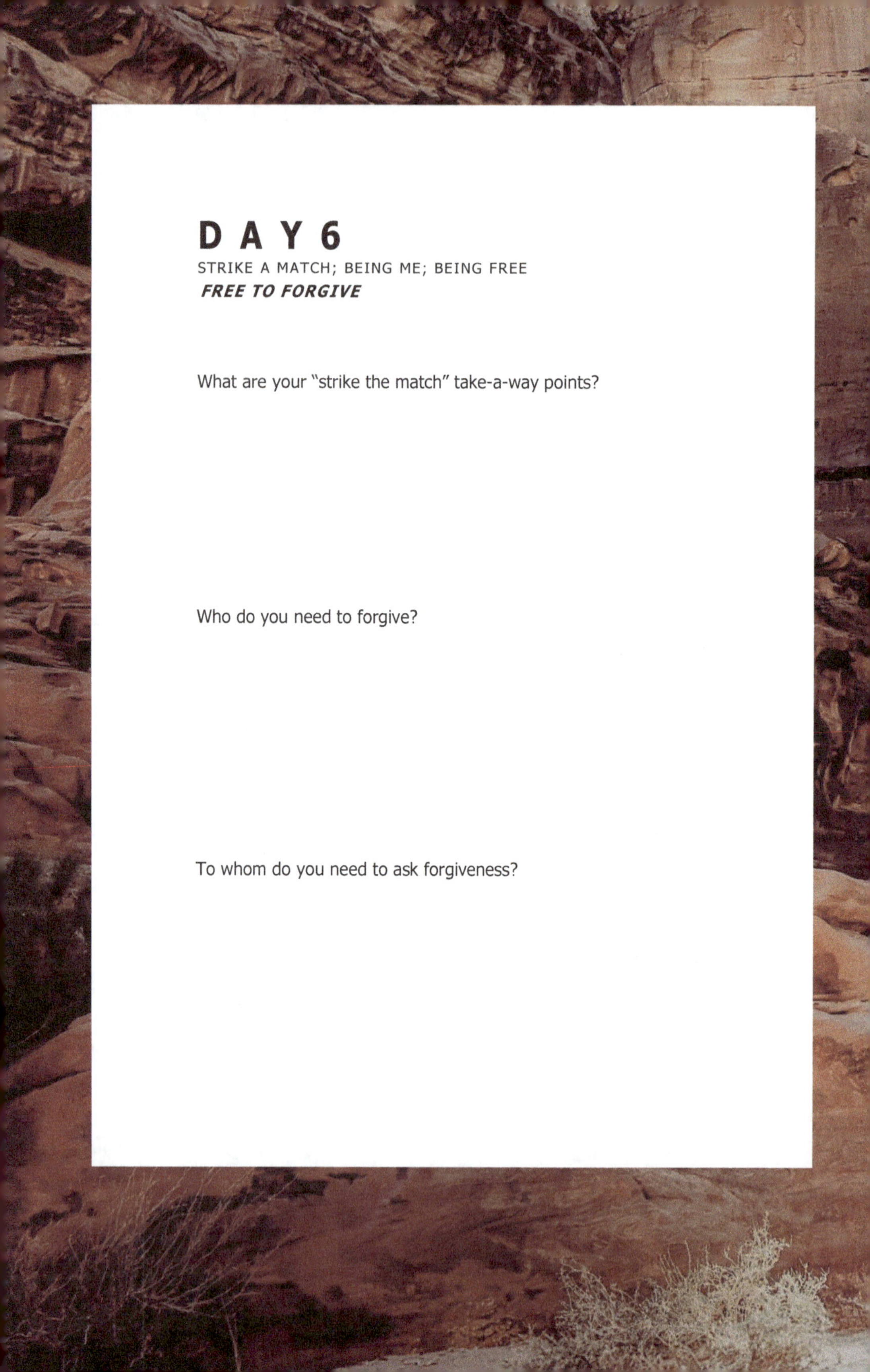

D A Y 6

FREE TO FORGIVE

What are your "strike the match" take-a-way points?

Who do you need to forgive?

To whom do you need to ask forgiveness?

FATHER (JACOB) WAS DEAD,
JOSEPH'S BROTHERS
BECAME FEARFUL...
SO THEY SENT THIS MESSAGE
TO JOSEPH: ...SO WE, THE
SERVANTS OF THE GOD OF
YOUR FATHER, BEG YOU TO
FORGIVE OUR SIN." WHEN
JOSEPH RECEIVED THE
MESSAGE, HE BROKE DOWN
AND WEPT. THEN HIS
BROTHERS CAME AND THREW
THEMSE LVES DOWN BEFORE
JOSEPH. "LOOK, WE ARE YOUR
SLAVES!" THEY SAID.

BUT JOSEPH REPLIED, "DON'T
BE AFRAID OF ME. AM I GOD
THAT I CAN PUNISH YOU? YOU
INTENDED TO HARM ME, BUT
GOD INTENDED IT ALL FOR
GOOD. HE BROUGHT ME TO
THIS POSITION SO I COULD
SAVE THE LIVES OF MANY
PEOPLE. NO, DON'T BE
AFRAID. I WILL CONTINUE TO
TAKE CARE OF YOU AND YOUR
CHILDREN." SO HE
REASSURED THEM BY
SPEAKING KINDLY TO THEM.

Genesis 50:15-21

BEING ME; BEING FREE
DAY6 | *FREE TO FORGIVE,*

Dear Lord,

"Love is the greatest gift that God has given us. It's free."

-Taraji P. Henson

DAY 7
STRIKE A MATCH; BEING ME; BEING FREE
FREE TO LOVE

Being me is being free; I am free to be me, the me God has created me to be. I let go of the thoughts and things that hold me back, and I embrace being me; I am free.

We all love a good love story. This is a little different from The Notebook (arguably the best love story chick flick ever made), but this is a great story of support, devotion and love between two women, Ruth and Naomi. Ruth, a Moabite, married one of Naomi's (an Israelite) two sons. Ruth embraced her husband's family and faith, two cultures collided, and it worked because they made it work, until tragedy made an appearance. Naomi's husband passed away, then shortly after, both of her sons also passed.

These tragic events left three mourning widows, Naomi, Ruth and Orphah. All faced financial burdens, safety concerns, and decisions that needed to be made. Naomi, in her grief and as the matriarch, tried to make sense of the next steps. She announces, "Girls, you need to go back to your parents; I can't take care of you. Hopefully, you can find a path and a future despite all that has been lost" (loose quotation and bible translation).

She was trying her best to be selfless and give loving guidance, but her biggest concern was probably, "Who is going to take care of me now? My family is gone". Orphah heeded her mother-in-law's advice, and in tears, she said goodbye, but Ruth clung tightly to Naomi.

Strike A Match, Ruth was motivated by something greater than circumstance and convenience, she was motivated by love, love for her mother-in-law, Naomi. Ruth vowed, "Wherever you go, I will go; wherever you live, I will live. Your people will be my people, and your God will be my God". These two women of great character honored and supported each other in every aspect of life.

Ruth traveled home with Naomi to Bethlehem, where she met a man, Boaz, who redeemed the family, giving a secure future to the next generation. Ruth was free to love with all her heart. She loved despite loss, she loved despite heartbreak, she loved despite uncertainty, and she eventually was able to love again, have children and become the great-grandmother of King David.

"Love never fails" makes great wall decor; hang it up, display it as a home motto, but do we really live it? In a world where a guarded heart is a heart that cannot be broken, the safest choice seems to be to love protected, like it is a matter of national security. It is as if anytime a part of our heart gets broken, we take that piece and wrap it up in an emotional Kevlar safe so it can never again be assaulted, but at what cost? What is forfeited?

In that locked-up place, the heart is not free to love because it remains defined by the inflicted wound. Hurt did not define Ruth's heart, and it doesn't define yours. Ruth chose to love greater, not guarded. She chose to recognize God's love for her would never fail, so when Ruth chose love, she knew she would not fail. Your love story, despite heartbreak, loss, and uncertainty, is still being written. Your heart will be known by your capacity to love greater.

You can love freely, knowing that love never fails and you will not fail when you allow your whole heart to love. You are free, free to love greater. "Being me is being free; I am free to be me, the me God has created me to be. I let go of the thoughts and things that hold me back, and I embrace being me; I am free."

D A Y 7

STRIKE A MATCH; BEING ME; BEING FREE
FREE TO LOVE

What are your "strike the match" take-a-way points?

Which parts of your heart do you need to release from an emotional safe?

How will you love greater today?

BUT ON THE WAY, NAOMI SAID TO HER TWO DAUGHTERS-IN-LAW, "GO BACK TO YOUR MOTHERS' HOMES. AND MAY THE LORD REWARD YOU FOR YOUR KINDNESS TO YOUR HUSBANDS AND TO ME. MAY THE LORD BLESS YOU WITH THE SECURITY OF ANOTHER MARRIAGE." THEN SHE KISSED THEM GOODBYE, AND THEY ALL BROKE DOWN AND WEPT……AND AGAIN, THEY WEPT TOGETHER, AND ORPAH KISSED HER MOTHER-IN-LAW GOODBYE. BUT RUTH CLUNG TIGHTLY TO NAOMI. "LOOK," NAOMI SAID TO HER, "YOUR SISTER-IN-LAW HAS GONE BACK TO HER PEOPLE AND TO HER GODS. YOU SHOULD DO THE SAME. "BUT RUTH REPLIED, "DON'T ASK ME TO LEAVE YOU AND TURN BACK. WHEREVER YOU GO, I WILL GO; WHEREVER YOU LIVE, I WILL LIVE. YOUR PEOPLE WILL BE MY PEOPLE, AND YOUR GOD WILL BE MY GOD. WHEREVER YOU DIE, I WILL DIE, AND THERE I WILL BE BURIED. MAY THE LORD PUNISH ME SEVERELY IF I ALLOW ANYTHING BUT DEATH TO SEPARATE US!" WHEN NAOMI SAW THAT RUTH WAS DETERMINED TO GO WITH HER, SHE SAID NOTHING MORE.

Ruth 1:8-9,14-18

BEING ME; BEING FREE
DAY 7 | *FREE TO LOVE*

90

Dear Lord,

PART 3

BEING ME; **BEING LOVE**

STRIKE A MATCH DEVOTION

The catalyst to starting a fire in my soul

STRIKE
/strik/
To ignite, to produce a spark;

MATCH
/maCH/
A simple tool used to create a spark to start a fire.

DEVOTION
/dəˈvōSH(ə)n/
An observance that can include prayer, reading, and writing.
A source of reflective thoughtfulness to improve one's well-being.

LOVE
/luv/
An intense feeling of deep affection. The act of giving selflessly to someone else, with their best interest and wellbeing being a priority

BEING ME; BEING LOVE

Being me is being love. I possess the unhindered ability to love. True love is the foundation of all that is good, and I can receive love, freely give love and be a love light, an example of all that is good.

Being me is being love.

"Love does not dominate; it cultivates."
-Johann Wolfgang von Goethe

D A Y 1
STRIKE A MATCH; BEING ME; BEING LOVE
CULTIVATING LOVE

Being me is being love. I possess the unhindered ability to love. True love is the foundation of all that is good. I can receive love and freely give love. I am a love light, an example of all that is good. Being me is being love.

Everyone loves a good story, the funniest or the most embarrassing stories usually start out, "Do you remember that one time?" The New Testament is partially a historical account of "Do you remember that one time?" moments are written about one of the greatest storytellers to ever walk the earth, Jesus Christ.

So good, He would have had his own TED Talk, or millions of followers on Instagram. He had this amazing ability to weave thought-provoking truth into every part of his lake shore or street corner, crowd-gathering narratives, and those closest to him took notes.

Matthew picks up his papyrus pen and begins to write it all down (poetic license version of Matthew's account coming up). One time, there was a farmer in a field. It was a beautiful late spring morning; the sun had just come up, darkness scattered, and the coolness of the morning gave way to the warmth of day.

He was carrying a bag across his chest full of seeds, and it was time to plant. Little did he know the challenges he would face germinating his crop. His seed was premium, but could it take root and grow?

Everywhere the farmer went in his field, he freely gave the seed to the earth. He spread it along the path, in the rocky soil, among the thorns, and others fell into the heart of the field. The seed never changed, but the placement of the seed was vital. Most of the seeds met a tragic fate because the earth was not able to embrace the potential of seeds.

However, the farmer was successful in the heart of the field, where the soil was cultivated, suitable for the premium seed to take root and grow. **Strike A Match**: are we talking about corn, wheat or something else? What is the storyteller trying to say? Who is this farmer, and what is he truly trying to plant? The crowds were as baffled as those closest to Jesus. His purpose was to provoke spiritual thinking by giving a practical example. The farmer, God. The God of the universe, of creation, of time, space and wisdom, is planting his word. His word, the premium love seeds that are freely scattered upon the earth that can take root and grow in the field hearts of the people of the world.

We all have a love story to tell. It may or may not involve an actual farmer, but yours fits into one of the four genres, as do all the love stories repeated since the beginning of time. 1) When love was snatched or flew away (seed along the path), or 2) when it sprang up quickly but then died because it was superficial or immature (seed in rocky soil), or 3) when it was deceit disguised as love (seed in the thorns) or lastly 4) true love.

We have been either witness to or the owner of poor soil that the premium seed of God's word, the author of true love, could not take root and grow as God intended it to flourish. It is tragic the love that has been lost, that has not taken root because of hurt in the soil of people's hearts. But now is your time, your "remember that one time moment" when the darkness has scattered, and the coolness is giving way to warmth.

Your time for the farmer, God, to plant in your heart a new understanding of His word and true love. Your heart is ready when you choose it to be ready when you choose to embrace the potential of the seed He is freely giving. He chooses you to cultivate His love throughout the earth; it is time for your heart to let that seed take root and grow unhindered. I am cultivating love. Being me is being loved. I possess the unhindered ability to love. True love is the foundation of all that is good. I can receive love and freely give love. I am a love light, an example of all that is good. Being me is being loved.

D A Y 1

STRIKE A MATCH; BEING ME; BEING LOVE
CULTIVATING LOVE

What are your "strike the match" take-a-way points?

What does it mean to you that you are meant to be God's good soil?

How will you embrace the potential of the farmer's seed in your life today?

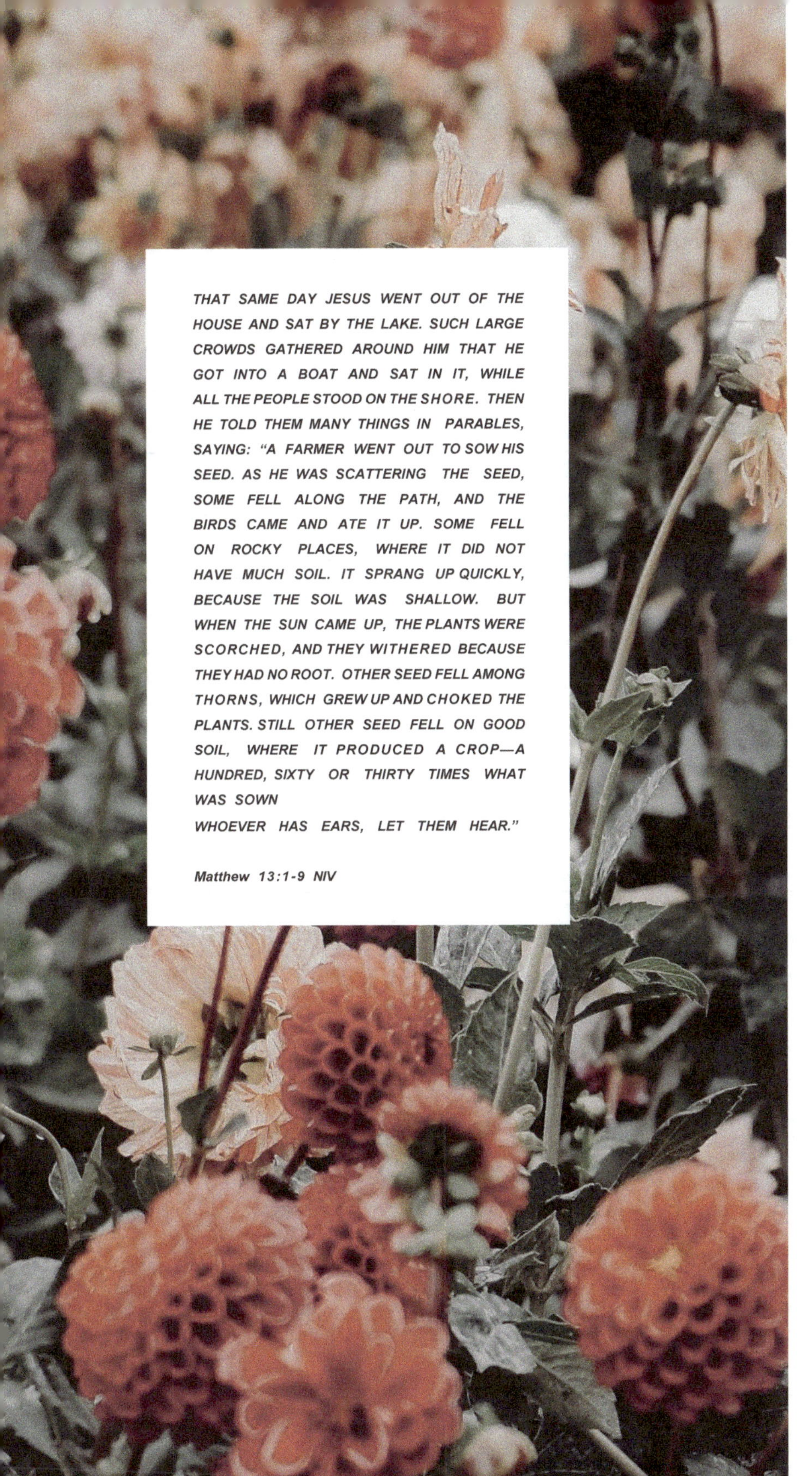

THAT SAME DAY JESUS WENT OUT OF THE HOUSE AND SAT BY THE LAKE. SUCH LARGE CROWDS GATHERED AROUND HIM THAT HE GOT INTO A BOAT AND SAT IN IT, WHILE ALL THE PEOPLE STOOD ON THE SHORE. THEN HE TOLD THEM MANY THINGS IN PARABLES, SAYING: "A FARMER WENT OUT TO SOW HIS SEED. AS HE WAS SCATTERING THE SEED, SOME FELL ALONG THE PATH, AND THE BIRDS CAME AND ATE IT UP. SOME FELL ON ROCKY PLACES, WHERE IT DID NOT HAVE MUCH SOIL. IT SPRANG UP QUICKLY, BECAUSE THE SOIL WAS SHALLOW. BUT WHEN THE SUN CAME UP, THE PLANTS WERE SCORCHED, AND THEY WITHERED BECAUSE THEY HAD NO ROOT. OTHER SEED FELL AMONG THORNS, WHICH GREW UP AND CHOKED THE PLANTS. STILL OTHER SEED FELL ON GOOD SOIL, WHERE IT PRODUCED A CROP—A HUNDRED, SIXTY OR THIRTY TIMES WHAT WAS SOWN
WHOEVER HAS EARS, LET THEM HEAR."

Matthew 13:1-9 NIV

BEING ME, BEING LOVE
DAY 1 | *CULTIVATING LOVE*

Dear Lord,

____

____

____

____

____

____

____

____

____

____

____

"The cure for all the ills and wrongs, the cares, the sorrows, and the crimes of humanity, all lie in the one word 'love'. It is the divine vitality that everywhere produces and restores life."

-Lydia M. Child

D A Y 2
STRIKE A MATCH; BEING ME; BEING LOVE
DIVINELY LOVED

Being me is being love. I possess the unhindered ability to love. True love is the foundation of all that is good. I can receive love and freely give love. I am a love light, an example of all that is good. Being me is being love.

Who me, are you asking me to join you, leave my boat, the sea and my catch of the day? Little did John, the fisherman, know he was the catch of the day along with his brother James. Jesus was telling stories on the shore, and the next thing John knew, he was trading his nets for the unknown. His heart sparked, and his mind was captured by thought-provoking truth, sound familiar?

John's life was not easy; he could have been a guest on "Dirty Jobs", and he could have been interviewed in a docu-series called "Romans, Living under a Militant Government Regime". John could have starred in his own TV series, "AD Camping" or "Island Life" for all the nights he spent sleeping under the skies or exiled in a cave on the Island of Patmos.

He was the witness to many miracles, the most miraculous, seeing first hand a resurrected Jesus. So many crazy things in his life that he should write a book; guess what? He did. John wrote 5 books of the Bible, including the wrap-up book, Revelations. Everything he did was noteworthy, but he is remembered as John the Beloved. He referred to himself as "the disciple whom Jesus loved" five times in his writings.

It seems very presumptuous and almost arrogant to use a third-person phrase like that to describe yourself, but he boldly did. Why would anyone do that? He wrote about the great things that he did and saw with Jesus and the eleven other disciples, but did he realize that people all over the world, 2000 plus years later, would still be reading what he wrote? **Strike A Match**, the lives that have been impacted by the words he wrote are innumerable and he had no idea. He simply wanted to remember the blessed life that opened up to him the day he met Jesus. He marked himself as a special beloved, with a relationship of great depth, and he made it his identity. His identity was not based on any of the cool, crazy things he did or his bill-paying vocation. In his writings, he had to remind himself of the singular truth, "I am completely, perfectly loved by God". It wasn't arrogance, it was to call to mind what was real in his heart so that he would be able to live through the reality of life. By the time he started writing, most of the disciples, including his own brother, were martyrs for the message of Jesus Christ. He watched as Jesus was sentenced and crucified. John was the only disciple who died of natural causes. During that time, he was given and wrote the revelation of God. His life was remarkable and difficult, yet he defined and identified himself as perfectly and fully loved by God.

May I see your identification, please? We each then proceed to give a laminated hologram card with an awkward picture, birth date, height, weight, eye color and address to the requestee… Showing your identification is the only way you gain access to a multitude of things: boarding a plane, getting a job, opening a bank account, driving, buying a car or a house, adopting a pet, and the list goes on and on. At any moment, you have to be ready to share personal "specs", but it really doesn't tell anything about you and yet this is how most people define their "ID". John knew better; he knew his personal identification needed to be more than "specs", but it had to be rooted in something bigger, greater than he could comprehend divine love.

When John accepted the truth of divine love it gave him access, access to a personal perspective that fortified his soul for everything he faced in life. We are no different, and we have access to that same truth. Our souls need to be defined by divine love. Your identity, you also are "the one whom Jesus loved". You are perfectly and fully loved by God. You are divinely loved. Being me is being love. I possess the unhindered ability to love. True love is the foundation of all that is good. I can receive love and freely give love. I am a love light, an example of all that is good. Being me is being loved.

D A Y 2
STRIKE A MATCH; BEING ME; BEING LOVE
DIVINELY LOVED

What are your "strike the match" take-a-way points?

What does it mean to you that you are divinely loved?

How do you define your identity to fortify your soul?

NOW ON THE FIRST DAY OF THE WEEK MARY MAGDALENE CAME TO THE TOMB EARLY, WHILE IT WAS STILL DARK, AND SAW THAT THE STONE HAD BEEN TAKEN AWAY FROM THE TOMB. SO SHE RAN AND WENT TO SIMON PETER AND THE OTHER DISCIPLE, THE ONE WHOM JESUS LOVED, AND SAID TO THEM, "THEY HAVE TAKEN THE LORD OUT OF THE TOMB, AND WE DO NOT KNOW WHERE THEY HAVE LAID HIM." SO PETER WENT OUT WITH THE OTHER DISCIPLE, AND THEY WERE GOING TOWARD THE TOMB. BOTH OF THEM WERE RUNNING TOGETHER, BUT THE OTHER DISCIPLE OUTRAN PETER AND REACHED THE TOMB FIRST. AND STOOPING TO LOOK IN, HE SAW THE LINEN CLOTHES LYING THERE, BUT HE DID NOT GO IN.

JOHN 20:1-5

BEING ME, BEING LOVE
DAY 2 | *DIVINELY LOVED*

Dear Lord,

"Love is always bestowed as a gift – freely, willingly, and without expectation. We don't love to be loved; we love to love."

-Leo Buscaglia

DAY 3

STRIKE A MATCH; BEING ME; BEING LOVE

SURRENDERED LOVE

Being me is being love. I possess the unhindered ability to love. True love is the foundation of all that is good. I can receive love and freely give love. I am a love light, an example of all that is good. Being me is being love.

Dinner plans were set for a Wednesday evening. Simon, a highly regarded church official, had sent out the invite, and Jesus and the crew were going to his place for a manly talkfest and some wings(well, maybe not wings). The conversation, the food, and the company, all was going as planned until an interruption became awkward for everyone in the room, with the exception of Jesus and a certain woman named Mary.

She entered the home, and she made her way to the one that was the life of the party. The atmosphere in the room shifted; judging looks, thoughts and statements filled the room. This woman was known in the town of Bethany and maybe by some of the elite men in Simon's friend circle... She did not carry her iPhone, waiting for the perfect selfie moment, she didn't have in her hands Jesus' favorite homemade side dish, nor did she have her purse open to give an offering to the ministry, all of which would have been more acceptable in the eyes of the glaring guest.

This unwelcome party crasher had a different purpose. She carried an alabaster jar filled with pure nard, a very expensive perfume, and this possession tells us a lot about this woman. She was not poor, she was possibly a courtesan of her day, a kept mistress or a paid escort to those of influence, that she held such a valuable item in her hand. She broke the jar, poured out the perfume, and the fragrance filled the room. This was not on the agenda, but something Jesus said caused her to seize the moment, a moment to give from her heart, a heart that had been transformed. **Strike A Match**, she poured out the most valuable thing she possessed, it represented her past, present and future. The act of breaking and anointing the feet of Jesus was an unprecedented display of a heart completely surrendered, completely grateful, and completely overwhelmed by the pure love of the Messiah.

She offended everyone in the room; the religious leaders and the disciples were indignant to Mary and questioned Jesus. She did not care how she would be judged, and she didn't do it for them; she was done measuring worth by worldly standards. She saw his worth, and she poured it all out. Jesus saw her heart and His words about her, "Truly I tell you, wherever the gospel is preached throughout the world, what she has done will also be told, in memory of her." Her story of surrendered love is still being told.

At one time or another, we have all assessed things incorrectly, "No problem, sure the sofa will fit through the door and up the stairs", only to find out in the moments after that statement that our idealistic measurement is not reality and we find ourselves and a piece of furniture wedged between the levels of our home. After a lesson of that magnitude, we may insist on measuring everything once, twice, maybe 3 times so as to not miscalculate physical space ever again.

However, we measure out more than that. We measure our beauty by the perfect selfie, we measure our ingredients for the perfect homemade recipe, we measure our worth by the amount of money in our wallet, and we measure out what our heart is willing to give. We put a cap on our capacity to love, but for what purpose? What if we measured our life by the love that we poured out? Is that currency offensive? Is it detrimental? Is it scary? Only by the ones that do not understand the pure love of the Messiah.

We can look at our past in the light of that love and be grateful that we are still standing. We can look at our present in the light of that love to be one that seizes a moment. We can look at our future in the light of that love and know that surrendered love is not only giving love; it is a contribution to our life's love story, a story that will be remembered. "If you are still measuring out your offering, you haven't seen His worth. She (Mary) saw his worth, and she poured it all out"– Klaus. Being me is being love. I possess the unhindered ability to love. True love is the foundation of all that is good. I can receive love and freely give love. I am a love light, an example of all that is good. Being me is being loved.

D A Y 3

SURRENDERED LOVE

What are your "strike the match" take-a-way points?

What are the things in your life that you are still measuring out? Do you see the worth of surrendered love?

How do you personally define surrendered love in your life? Bonus Challenge– Listen to the song "Stay Amazed" by Klaus (featuring Elizabeth Clark).

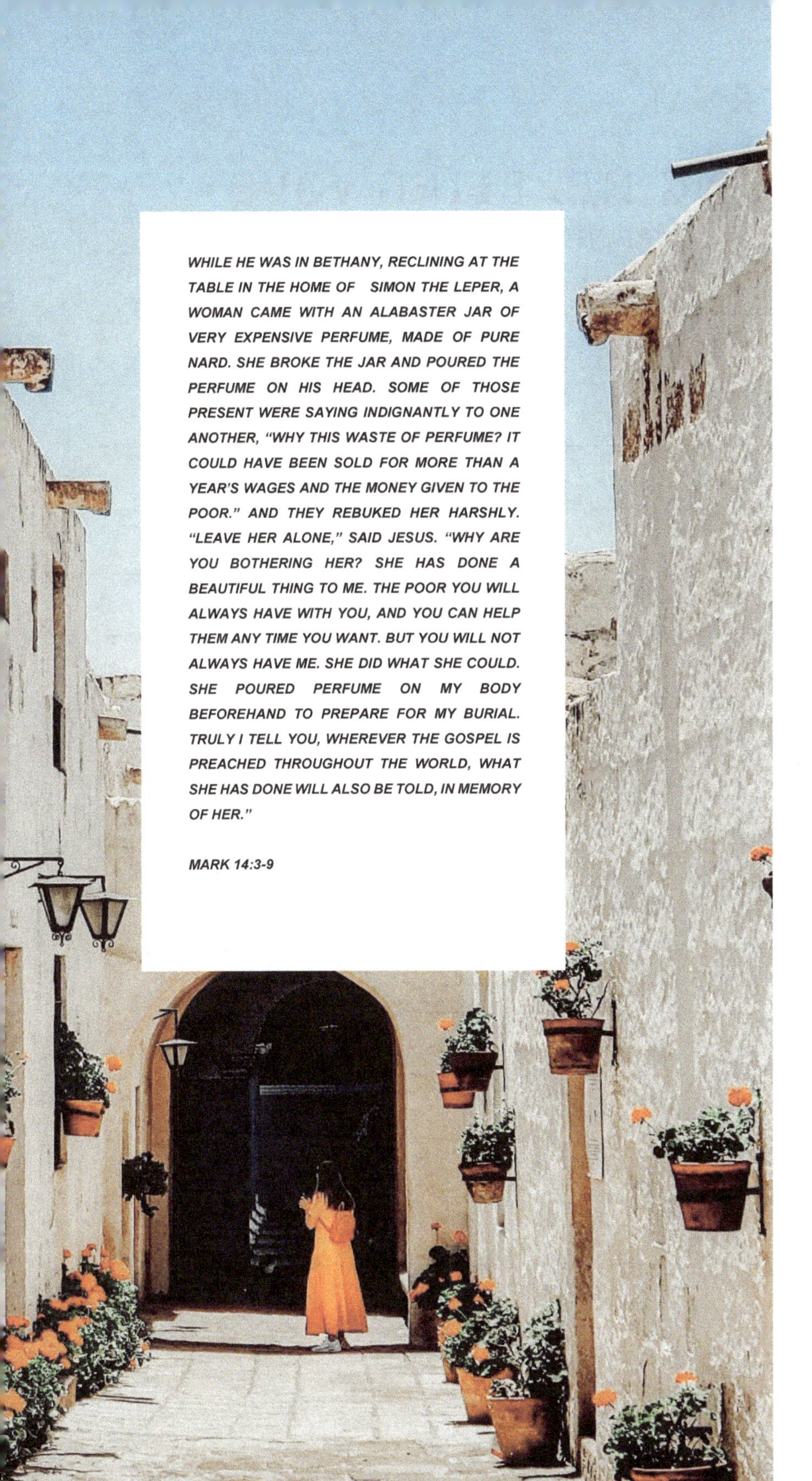

WHILE HE WAS IN BETHANY, RECLINING AT THE TABLE IN THE HOME OF SIMON THE LEPER, A WOMAN CAME WITH AN ALABASTER JAR OF VERY EXPENSIVE PERFUME, MADE OF PURE NARD. SHE BROKE THE JAR AND POURED THE PERFUME ON HIS HEAD. SOME OF THOSE PRESENT WERE SAYING INDIGNANTLY TO ONE ANOTHER, "WHY THIS WASTE OF PERFUME? IT COULD HAVE BEEN SOLD FOR MORE THAN A YEAR'S WAGES AND THE MONEY GIVEN TO THE POOR." AND THEY REBUKED HER HARSHLY. "LEAVE HER ALONE," SAID JESUS. "WHY ARE YOU BOTHERING HER? SHE HAS DONE A BEAUTIFUL THING TO ME. THE POOR YOU WILL ALWAYS HAVE WITH YOU, AND YOU CAN HELP THEM ANY TIME YOU WANT. BUT YOU WILL NOT ALWAYS HAVE ME. SHE DID WHAT SHE COULD. SHE POURED PERFUME ON MY BODY BEFOREHAND TO PREPARE FOR MY BURIAL. TRULY I TELL YOU, WHEREVER THE GOSPEL IS PREACHED THROUGHOUT THE WORLD, WHAT SHE HAS DONE WILL ALSO BE TOLD, IN MEMORY OF HER."

MARK 14:3-9

BEING ME, BEING LOVE
DAY 3 | *SURRENDERED LOVE*

Dear Lord,

"When you look into the depths of your soul, you see what God sees, an original created being, a perfectly flawed human with an eternal soul that is forgiven and fueled by love."

-S. Study

DAY 4
STRIKE A MATCH; BEING ME; BEING LOVE
SOULFUL LOVE

Being me is being love. I possess the unhindered ability to love. True love is the foundation of all that is good. I can receive love and freely give love. I am a love light, an example of all that is good. Being me is being loved.

Was it really a good Friday? The sentence was carried out, all hope gone. The chances of posting bail or getting paroled were no longer an option. Upon a hill full of spectators, soldiers, and mourners stood three wooden crosses. Each cross held a man, men all convicted of social crimes. Two of the men threatened the safety of the citizens, known thieves.

One of the men, Jesus, threatened the social norm, the corrupt establishment of government and religion, with a new and radical message. His radical message was not of mutiny, and it wasn't a revolution but a revelation of hope, forgiveness, and a heavenly kingdom for eternal souls. Was it a crime worthy of being placed between two criminals? That was the debate of the day dividing the on-lookers and also for the two men meeting the same fate as Jesus.

With heckling from the crowd and between agonizing breaths, the men on the crosses engaged in a profound dialog as if each thief represented opposing sides of the hilltop crucifixion debate. The one to the left was of the opinion, "Save me from the situation I have gotten myself into if you are really the Messiah". The other, to the right, thinks deeper, creating his opinion based on the bigger picture, the soulful level. The reality of the situation was not changing, but could he do one thing that would change the state of his soul? Could he take ownership of his actions, emotions, personal characteristics and his intellect at this moment? Could he embrace soulful love, forgive himself, accept forgiveness from the man in the middle, and reconcile his soul for the eternal prospect? **Strike A Match**, the encounter changed one of the thief's hearts in a moment, the material things he wrongfully sought after paled in comparison to the revelation of the radical message of Jesus; it became hope and peace, wiping away self-condemnation because he saw and realized the purpose of the man hanging upon the middle cross. He was making a way to a heavenly kingdom for the soulful.

The thieves represent the debate in our own minds. Most of us with a Christian faith have acknowledged and accepted the forgiveness that Jesus offers to us through the cross. But forgiveness is only half of the purpose of the cross, reconciliation is the other half. This reconciliation is soulful love; it is spiritual, between you and God; and it is internal, between you and yourself. "Soulful love is powerful, it is the love felt from the essence of your being — the fabric of your uniqueness'" (-Kim Petersen "Living Out Loud ").

The thief recognized, acknowledged and accepted the whole package at that moment, and so must we. To be forgiven is a gift of the cross. Did the thief deserve it, not in human eyes but in heavenly eyes? He did, and so do you. To forgive yourself is the acknowledgment that what Jesus did on the cross is more than enough. To say you cannot forgive yourself is not humble; it is denying the power of the soulful love of Jesus' sacrifice. If we can be forgiven by Him, we must be able to forgive ourselves; it is imperative to the health of our soul in this life and the eternal life to come. That is the soulful love package of the cross. Being me is being love. I possess the unhindered ability to love. True love is the foundation of all that is good. I can receive love and freely give love. I am a love light, an example of all that is good. Being me is being loved.

D A Y 4

SOULFUL LOVE

What are your "strike the match" take-a-way points?

What are the things you are struggling to forgive yourself for?

What does it mean to you to acknowledge and accept soulful love (complete forgiveness and reconciliation)?

JESUS SAID, "FATHER, FORGIVE THEM, FOR THEY DON'T KNOW WHAT THEY ARE DOING." AND THE SOLDIERS GAMBLED FOR HIS CLOTHES BY THROWING DICE. 35 THE CROWD WATCHED AND THE LEADERS SCOFFED. "HE SAVED OTHERS," THEY SAID, "LET HIM SAVE HIMSELF IF HE IS REALLY GOD'S MESSIAH, THE CHOSEN ONE." THE SOLDIERS MOCKED HIM, TOO, BY OFFERING HIM A DRINK OF SOUR WINE. THEY CALLED OUT TO HIM, "IF YOU ARE THE KING OF THE JEWS, SAVE YOURSELF!" A SIGN WAS FASTENED ABOVE HIM WITH THESE WORDS: "THIS IS THE KING OF THE JEWS." ONE OF THE CRIMINALS HANGING BESIDE HIM SCOFFED, "SO YOU'RE THE MESSIAH, ARE YOU? PROVE IT BY SAVING YOURSELF—AND US, TOO, WHILE YOU'RE AT IT!" BUT THE OTHER CRIMINAL PROTESTED, "DON'T YOU FEAR GOD EVEN WHEN YOU HAVE BEEN SENTENCED TO DIE? WE DESERVE TO DIE FOR OUR CRIMES, BUT THIS MAN HASN'T DONE ANYTHING WRONG." THEN HE SAID, "JESUS, REMEMBER ME WHEN YOU COME INTO YOUR KINGDOM." AND JESUS REPLIED, "I ASSURE YOU, TODAY YOU WILL BE WITH ME IN PARADISE."

LUKE 23:32-43 NLT

JOURNAL

BEING ME, BEING LOVE

DAY 4 | *SOULFUL LOVE*

Dear Lord,

"Loving others always costs us something and requires effort. And you have to decide to do it on purpose. You can't wait for a feeling to motivate you."

-Joyce Meyer

DAY 5
STRIKE A MATCH; BEING ME; BEING LOVE
ADHESIVE LOVE

Being me is being love. I possess the unhindered ability to love. True love is the foundation of all that is good. I can receive love and freely give love. I am a love light, an example of all that is good. Being me is being loved.

"This cannot be happening. I committed my heart, my life, my future, and this is what I get for being an upstanding citizen and devoted follower of God." This must have been the dialog in Joseph's mind, and nothing made sense! It all started with a glance and a smile, and he had found the woman he wanted to spend the rest of his life with. They were engaged and vowed to be pure until the day they would be married. All sounds very normal, but the bride-to-be, Mary, was hiding a scandalous secret of a divine nature.

During the betrothal, when all of the matrimonial preparations should have been made, Mary takes a three-month road trip to clear her head, gain understanding and find strength for her divine purpose as it was spoken to her by a messenger from God. When she returned to her hometown, Nazareth, she could no longer hide her secret. Mouths dropped and eyes glared as Mary walked down the street noticeably with a bun in the oven, and I don't mean baking bread.

The gossip tree caught fire, and now she faced the whispering fire squad of scandal, assumption and the perception of her unfaithfulness. The one it affected most was Joseph; he did nothing wrong, and it wasn't his fault she was walking around unwed and pregnant. He may have even said, "I don't know what happened, and I don't care; I'm out, engagement off". He may have said, "I have tried to be a good man, I tried to be faithful to the promise that was made, but I'm not trying anymore!" Traditions and the culture of the day allowed Joseph to publicly accuse Mary of the obvious betrayal and her vigilante sentence was a public stoning, rocks being thrown until death. Although hurt, Joseph's human thinking was merciful; he chose to privately dissolve the engagement so that a stoning would not take place, saving the life of Mary and the unborn child. It was a noble and honorable decision. However, little did he know it was just the beginning of his God-given purpose. Settled in his decision, one night, as Joseph slept, a great revelation came to him in a dream. The dream that was given to him explained how Mary was chosen to bring the son of God into the world and how Joseph, himself, was chosen to be a stepdad to that same baby, the very Messiah of the world. **Strike A Match**, every thought, hurt, and decision to walk away was now dissolved away by the clarity of God's purpose. Joseph's purpose was to recognize the love of God for the world and to stand with and love Mary in her God-given purpose. He was to be the glue of the family and to stick close to Mary. He was now "adhesive love," a deep, indescribable love marked by the heart of God's character, for the core purpose of radical reconciliation. God moved in the situation, and He answered all the doubts in a dream, and God's dream became the foundation of love in the heart of Joseph. God moved in the situation in a way that only He can do. Joseph embraced what God showed him, confidently went to Mary and took her hand in marriage. The task was not an easy one, but knowing God had a plan, he put everything aside to be the partner that Mary needed, he reconciled his relationship so that the world could be reconciled to God.

"Nope, not doing it; I have tried everything, this just isn't going to work! I don't care anymore; it just doesn't matter. Why should I take the first step? It's not my fault?" The same dialogue that Joseph may have had until God showed him the bigger picture is the same dialog we all struggle with when we do not see our situations as God does. The bigger picture, God's perspective, will give the knowledge that the heart needs to be adhesive love. For every relationship in your life, you have the choice to be the glue, and you have the choice to perpetuate reconciliation, not division. Why should you take the first step? Why shouldn't you? The first step is to ask God to see what He sees, to understand the situation, and then to give you the strength to embrace relationship reconciliation. The task may be more than you bargained for, but your pursuit of reconciliation may be the catalyst someone needs to be reconciled to God. You are adhesive love. Being me is being love. I possess the unhindered ability to love. True love is the foundation of all that is good. I can receive love and freely give love. I am a love light and an example of all that is good. Being me is being loved.

D A Y 5

What are your "strike the match" take-a-way points?

Which relationships in your life are struggling and need healing?

Ask God to see that situation/relationship as He does; what is He showing you?

THIS IS HOW THE BIRTH OF JESUS THE MESSIAH CAME ABOUT: HIS MOTHER MARY WAS PLEDGED TO BE MARRIED TO JOSEPH, BUT BEFORE THEY CAME TOGETHER, SHE WAS FOUND TO BE PREGNANT THROUGH THE HOLY SPIRIT. BECAUSE JOSEPH HER HUSBAND WAS FAITHFUL TO THE LAW, AND YET DID NOT WANT TO EXPOSE HER TO PUBLIC DISGRACE, HE HAD IN MIND TO DIVORCE HER QUIETLY. BUT AFTER HE HAD CONSIDERED THIS, AN ANGEL OF THE LORD APPEARED TO HIM IN A DREAM AND SAID, "JOSEPH SON OF DAVID, DO NOT BE AFRAID TO TAKE MARY HOME AS YOUR WIFE, BECAUSE WHAT IS CONCEIVED IN HER IS FROM THE HOLY SPIRIT. SHE WILL GIVE BIRTH TO A SON, AND YOU ARE TO GIVE HIM THE NAME JESUS, BECAUSE HE WILL SAVE HIS PEOPLE FROM THEIR SINS." ALL THIS TOOK PLACE TO FULFILL WHAT THE LORD HAD SAID THROUGH THE PROPHET: "THE VIRGIN WILL CONCEIVE AND GIVE BIRTH TO A SON, AND THEY WILL CALL HIM IMMANUEL" (WHICH MEANS "GOD WITH US"). WHEN JOSEPH WOKE UP, HE DID WHAT THE ANGEL OF THE LORD HAD COMMANDED HIM AND TOOK MARY HOME AS HIS WIFE. BUT HE DID NOT CONSUMMATE THEIR MARRIAGE UNTIL SHE GAVE BIRTH TO A SON. AND HE GAVE HIM THE NAME JESUS.

MATTHEW 1:18-24 NIV

BEING ME, BEING LOVE
DAY 5 | *ADHESIVE LOVE*

Dear Lord,

____

____

____

____

____

____

____

____

____

____

____

"To love another person is to see the face of God."

- Victor Hugo

DAY 6
STRIKE A MATCH; BEING ME; BEING LOVE
UNSPOKEN LOVE

Being me is being loved. I possess the unhindered ability to love. True love is the foundation of all that is good. I can receive love and freely give love. I am a love light, an example of all that is good. Being me is being love.

Seeing is believing, or is believing seeing? Two men walk into a house… not the beginning of a bad joke but the beginning of something completely different. The two men, friends because of a commonality, had an everyday struggle to sustain the basics of life; they were destitute and had very little hope for a future any different from their current circumstances. However, one day, they found themselves at the right place at the right time. It was a familiar place, but this day, someone different was at the house to talk to, Jesus. These men couldn't see the man they were talking to, physically blind, and they had been navigating life not knowing the magnificence of a sunrise, a sunset, the colors of the rainbow or their reflection in the mirror. Even though they were blind, they saw an opportunity. They were desperate enough to call out to Jesus, "Have mercy on us, Son of David!" They saw the opportunity, and He took the time to see them. He did not overlook those that society had turned a blind eye to. He engaged in a heart dialogue before he addressed their obvious struggle, the things that were hindering their hope for the future. "Do you believe I am able to do this?" was the question. Their faith was being challenged and their hearts were being unlocked by a simple inquiry.

Strike A Match, Jesus didn't ask because he wanted the attention or status, he asked because it was about connecting with people where they are, with what they are dealing with, and helping them see differently. He did not give judging words but instead gave action to His love. It was an unspoken display of love, stunningly beautiful and completely life-changing. These men would never be the same. Jesus saw them when they couldn't see themselves. Their eyes were opened to the world and to the face of God, and their hearts were flooded by the unspoken love of Jesus. They could not keep that day's event quiet, and nothing could hinder the joy of the encounter. Their new sight became their new story. Two men walked out of a house... thoroughly changed and telling all that would listen about someone different who found them in darkness and showed them love light.

We are given a great privilege: to be a love light. What if the main purpose and mission on this earth is to help those who do not understand or that cannot see clearly to be, as Jesus was, unspoken love? To be that someone different shows something different to those who have not seen the magnificent love of God. To ask some hard questions, "Do you believe that God can turn your situation around?" Mother Theresa said it best, "Spread love everywhere you go. Let no one ever come to you without leaving happier." We are to be that breath of fresh air, the revealer of how the soul can see the face of God. We are not to judge but to help people see a reflection of themselves that they are too broken to see. To be unspoken, love in action is what we were created to be. Being me is being love. I possess the unhindered ability to love. True love is the foundation of all that is good. I can receive love and freely give love. I am a love light, an example of all that is good. Being me is being love.

D A Y 6

STRIKE A MATCH; BEING ME; BEING LOVE
UNSPOKEN LOVE

What are your "strike the match" take-a-way points?

Is there someone that you know who needs to know something completely different, who needs help seeing themselves, the reflection through the face of God?

How can you be unspoken love today?

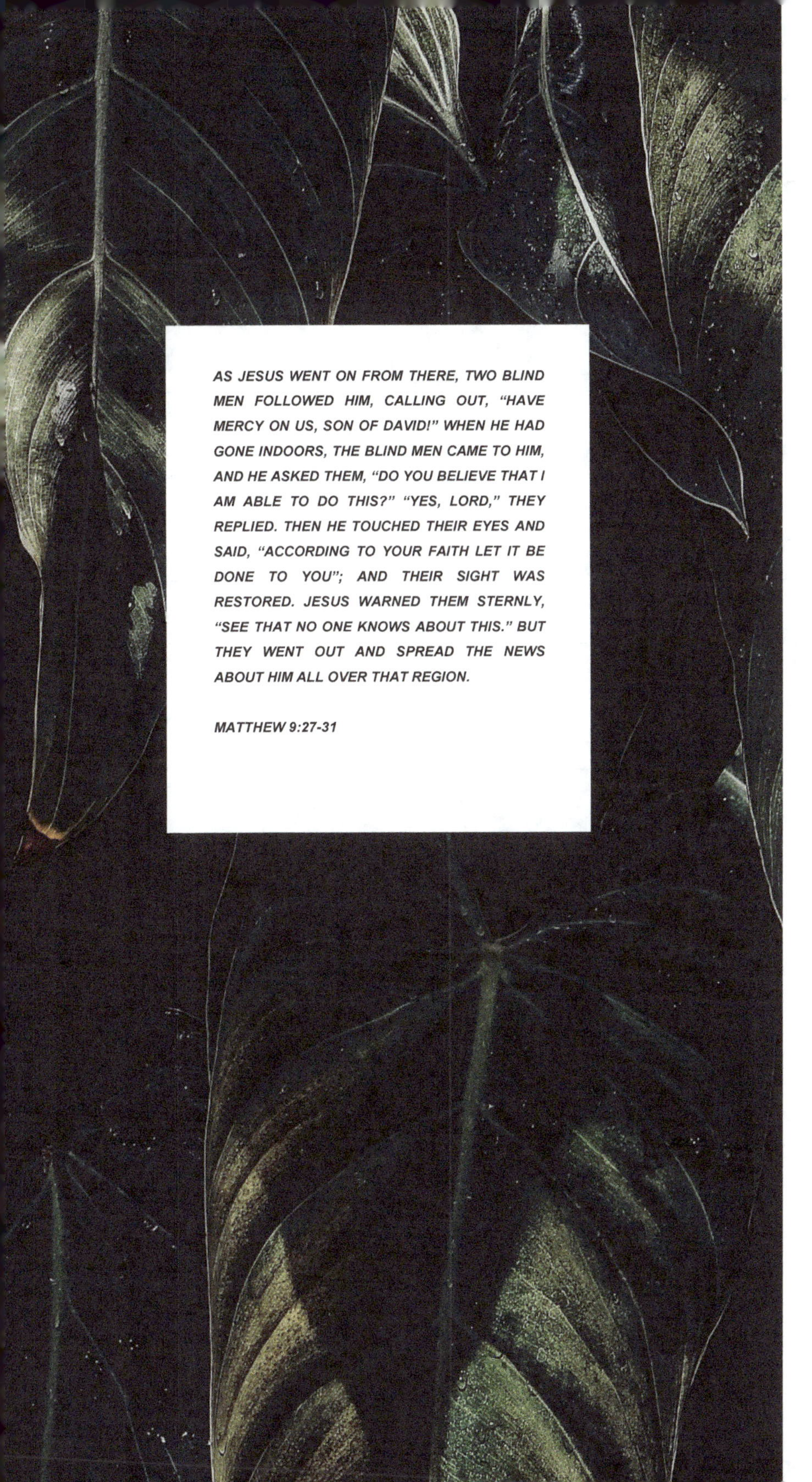

AS JESUS WENT ON FROM THERE, TWO BLIND MEN FOLLOWED HIM, CALLING OUT, "HAVE MERCY ON US, SON OF DAVID!" WHEN HE HAD GONE INDOORS, THE BLIND MEN CAME TO HIM, AND HE ASKED THEM, "DO YOU BELIEVE THAT I AM ABLE TO DO THIS?" "YES, LORD," THEY REPLIED. THEN HE TOUCHED THEIR EYES AND SAID, "ACCORDING TO YOUR FAITH LET IT BE DONE TO YOU"; AND THEIR SIGHT WAS RESTORED. JESUS WARNED THEM STERNLY, "SEE THAT NO ONE KNOWS ABOUT THIS." BUT THEY WENT OUT AND SPREAD THE NEWS ABOUT HIM ALL OVER THAT REGION.

MATTHEW 9:27-31

JOURNAL

BEING ME, BEING LOVE

DAY 6 | *UNSPOKEN LOVE*

Dear Lord,

"Someday, after mastering the winds, the waves, the tides and gravity, we shall harness for God the energies of love, and then, for a second time in the history of the world, man will have discovered fire."

- Pierre Teilhard de Chardin

D A Y 7
STRIKE A MATCH; BEING ME; BEING LOVE
LOVE WARRIOR

Being me is being loved. I possess the unhindered ability to love. True love is the foundation of all that is good. I can receive love and freely give love. I am a love light, an example of all that is good. Being me is being love.

Well, I guess he got knocked off his high horse. More than a saying, it actually happened to a prominent religious leader. Traveling to Damascus, this pharisee, on a mission to shut down the new gospel that had caught fire and threatened the traditions of his faith, had a light-flashing radical revelation (Acts 9). Saul, a great leader of the written law and his Jewish heritage, felt justified in the harsh and violent persecutions of those who had turned from acceptable observances to what was being labeled "good news" and "Christianity". The whole world seemed to be on fire politically and in the realm of established doctrine, and he was going to make things right again with his tenacious warrior spirit. That all changed in a flash along the road when the light from heaven caused him to fall off his horse and to be blind for 3 days. God got his attention, and it impacted him far deeper than physical wounds; it was a divine encounter that caused his warrior spirit to be redirected. His temporary blindness allowed him to see an eternal loving God, and from that moment on, Saul changed his name to Paul and changed his mission. He became a warrior spokesperson for the love of God, and the Jesus movement he once persecuted became the passion he pursued. Although it was not an easy journey, he was whipped, stoned (real rocks, not weed), shipwrecked, and imprisoned seven times. Paul's persistence did not fail in the tough times. He established at least fourteen different churches and wrote half of the New Testament of the Bible. From his prison cell, he wrote letters of encouragement and loving discipline to the churches; nothing stopped him from impacting the lives of many people.

Those letters are still capturing the heart of the reader to this day, many generations removed from when he scribed God inspired words from his spirit. Paul, despite everything he had done, despite any circumstance he found himself in, he fought as a warrior for a great love because of the cause of Christ.

Strike A Match, you are a warrior, you are a fighter, you have overcome so many things, and nothing can stop you from positively impacting the lives of many people. But, what are you fighting for? What are you a warrior of? At one time, Paul was fighting the wrong battle, persecuting people, trying to control and prove a religious point until a God encounter sparked a fire, a fire that showed him a new way to be a warrior. As we evaluate our own lives, how many times have we fought battles out of anger, jealousy, bitterness, insecurity, selfishness, trying to prove a point? Those are the wrong battles. We are supposed to be strong in the Lord, not fighting against flesh and blood but against those things that oppose love. How can that be done? Take the truths that you have ingested these last 20 days, and make it your armor, knowing that God is always fighting for you. Remember you are good enough, significant enough, strong enough, confident enough, qualified enough, wise enough, and crazy enough to fight the good fight. You are free to be you, to be seen, to be bold, and to dream. You are free from fear, free to forgive and free to love. You are a warrior of love, and you will be guided by God's spirit, stand firm in truth, walk by faith and be an agent of peace and love. You possess a '**Strike A Match**' spark that will enable you to discover a God-given fire deep within your soul for your life journey. Being me is being loved. I possess the unhindered ability to love. True love is the foundation of all that is good. I can receive love and freely give love. I am a love light, an example of all that is good. Being me is being loved.

D A Y 7

STRIKE A MATCH; BEING ME; BEING LOVE
LOVE WARRIOR

What are your "strike the match" take-a-way points?

What are you fighting for?

Why is it important for you to be a warrior of love and what you are fighting for?

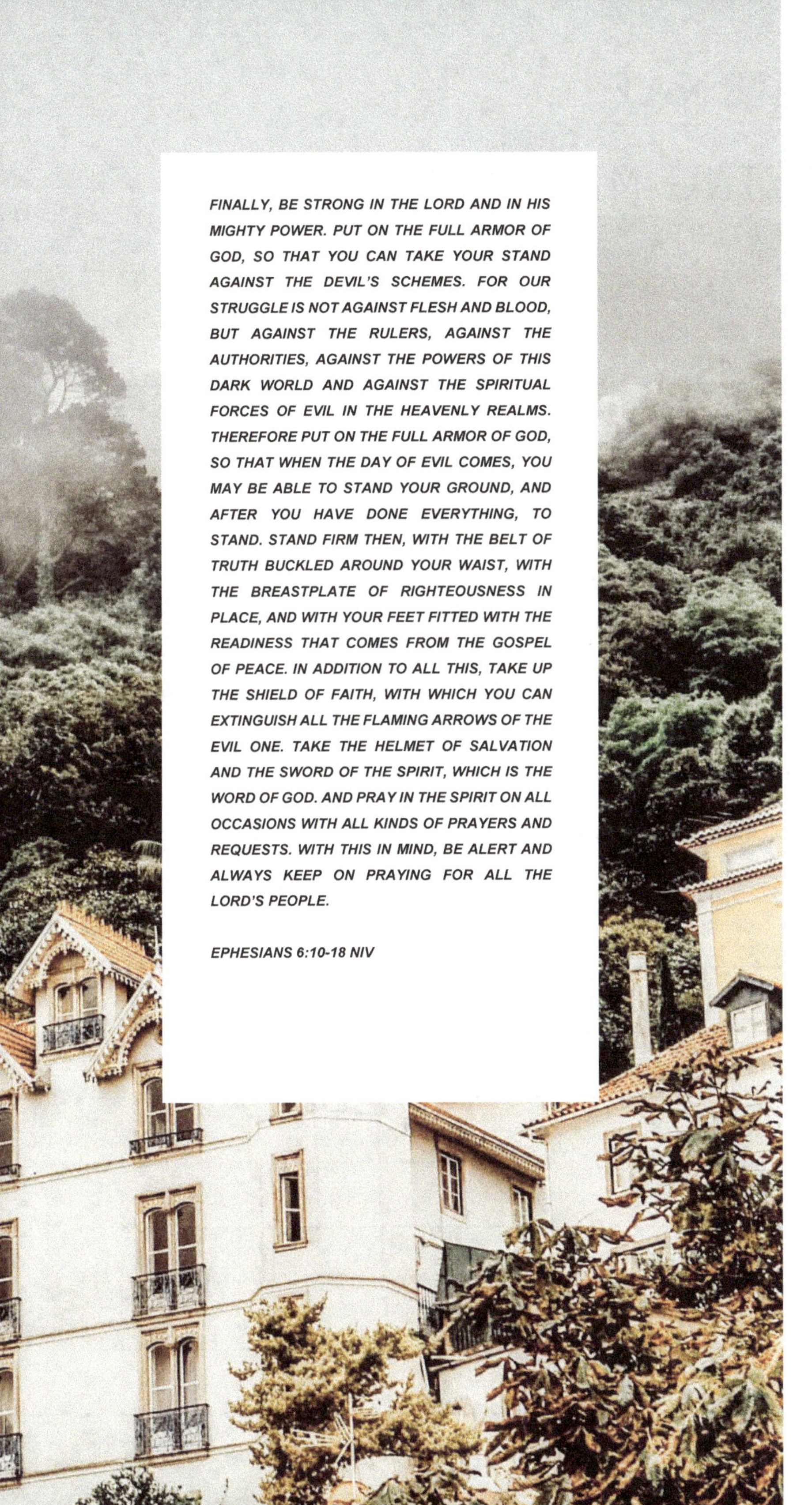

FINALLY, BE STRONG IN THE LORD AND IN HIS MIGHTY POWER. PUT ON THE FULL ARMOR OF GOD, SO THAT YOU CAN TAKE YOUR STAND AGAINST THE DEVIL'S SCHEMES. FOR OUR STRUGGLE IS NOT AGAINST FLESH AND BLOOD, BUT AGAINST THE RULERS, AGAINST THE AUTHORITIES, AGAINST THE POWERS OF THIS DARK WORLD AND AGAINST THE SPIRITUAL FORCES OF EVIL IN THE HEAVENLY REALMS. THEREFORE PUT ON THE FULL ARMOR OF GOD, SO THAT WHEN THE DAY OF EVIL COMES, YOU MAY BE ABLE TO STAND YOUR GROUND, AND AFTER YOU HAVE DONE EVERYTHING, TO STAND. STAND FIRM THEN, WITH THE BELT OF TRUTH BUCKLED AROUND YOUR WAIST, WITH THE BREASTPLATE OF RIGHTEOUSNESS IN PLACE, AND WITH YOUR FEET FITTED WITH THE READINESS THAT COMES FROM THE GOSPEL OF PEACE. IN ADDITION TO ALL THIS, TAKE UP THE SHIELD OF FAITH, WITH WHICH YOU CAN EXTINGUISH ALL THE FLAMING ARROWS OF THE EVIL ONE. TAKE THE HELMET OF SALVATION AND THE SWORD OF THE SPIRIT, WHICH IS THE WORD OF GOD. AND PRAY IN THE SPIRIT ON ALL OCCASIONS WITH ALL KINDS OF PRAYERS AND REQUESTS. WITH THIS IN MIND, BE ALERT AND ALWAYS KEEP ON PRAYING FOR ALL THE LORD'S PEOPLE.

EPHESIANS 6:10-18 NIV

BEING ME, BEING LOVE
DAY 7 | *LOVE WARRIOR*

Dear Lord,

READER QUOTES

"I enjoyed reading and contemplating the daily devotionals. They are an expression of faith and love for humanity"-CB.

"The devotion is beautiful, and it really made me think of my life in a much deeper, inner place." - BD

"What was most impactful for me was just being open and giving myself the personal space and time to spend in this devotional...I was moved and freed from burdens I had been carrying." – TM.

"Each day gave me food for thought, in ways I had never thought of before." – TL.

"Each week was relatable to those seeking recovery, starting with self-worth, finding freedom, and being directed to the true source of love." - JG.

"Encouraging..., the way the Bible stories and characters relate to modern-day situations, helps the reader to look at their trials from God's perspective and to put a different lens when looking at tough experiences or negative thoughts." -JO.

"I really enjoyed the devotionals...they had humor, and the biblical stories were related to modern-day times. I liked that they were short (manageable with a busy schedule)." - TS.

"Each week was its own journey that came together as a whole." - BB
"Well done! This devotion will make a difference in many lives." - DM
"I was excited each day to see where God would lead me." - BF
"This was a reminder of God's unwavering presence and faithfulness" - LG